THE FIRST LEGION

THE FIRST LEGION

A Drama of the Society of Jesus

BY

EMMET LAVERY

"Let others conquer the world. . . . even
as Alexander. . . . for us something more
is required. . . . it is for us to conquer
ourselves."—

FATHER RECTOR

ST. FRANCIS SEMINARY
SALZMANN
LIBRARY
MILWAUKEE 7, WIS.

SAMUEL FRENCH

NEW YORK   LOS ANGELES

SAMUEL FRENCH LTD.   LONDON

1934

ALL RIGHTS RESERVED

Copyright, 1933, 1934, by Emmet Lavery

CAUTION: Professionals and amateurs are hereby warned that "THE FIRST LEGION," being fully protected under the copyright laws of the United States of America, the British Empire, including the Dominion of Canada, and all other countries of the Copyright Union, is subject to royalty. All rights, including professional, amateur, motion pictures, recitation, public reading, radio broadcasting, and the rights of translation into foreign languages are strictly reserved. In its present form this play is dedicated to the reading public only. All inquiries regarding this play should be addressed to Samuel French at 25 West 45th Street, New York, N. Y., or at 811 West 7th Street, Los Angeles, Calif.

MANUFACTURED IN THE UNITED STATES OF AMERICA
BY THE VAIL-BALLOU PRESS, INC., BINGHAMTON, N. Y.

To Deborah

A. M. D. G.

Presented for the first time by BERT LYTELL and
PHIL GREEN on Monday, October 1, 1934, at the 46th
Street Theatre, New York, with the following cast:

"THE FIRST LEGION"

A DRAMA OF THE SOCIETY OF JESUS

By EMMET LAVERY

DIRECTED BY ANTHONY BROWN
SETTINGS BY EDWARD EDDY

REV. PAUL DUQESNE, S.J.................*William Ingersoll*

REV. CHARLES I. KEENE, S.J...................*Philip Wood*

REV. ROBERT STUART, S. J..................*Thomas Findlay*

DR. PETER MORELL........................*Harlan Tucker*

REV. EDWARD QUARTERMAN, S.J.............*Charles Coburn*

REV. MARK AHERN, S.J........................*Bert Lytell*

REV. THOMAS RAWLEIGH, S.J...................*John Litell*

REV. JOHN FULTON, S.J...................*Harold Moulton*

RT. REV. MONSIGNOR MICHAEL CAREY.......*Whitford Kane*

REV. JOSÉ MARIA SIERRA, S.J.............*Pedro de Cordoba*

JIMMY MAGEE.....................*Frank M. Thomas, Jr.*

Novices and Choir played by: Charles Danforth, John J.
Williams, Thomas Ewell, Joseph Fitzmaurice, Joseph Mitch-
ell, Jules Schmidt, Lester Atwell, Bruce Parish, Robert Pay-
son, Harry Lane, John Foster, Tom Monahan, Raymond
Wolber, Jerome Thor, Robert Barrett, Rob Wood, Wayne
Nelson, Frank Ray, Donald Wilson and Donald Barrie.

Choral and organ music under the supervision
of Father Finn, assisted by the senior chanters
of the Paulist Choir.

SCENES

NOTE

The "cell" like rooms of the priests are identical and can be inset within the great hall, if the fireplace side of the main set is mounted on rubber rollers for an easy swing back.

The music used in the play is on records at the Victor Company in New York—especially made for this production. A music chart of those records is part of this manuscript.

The confession scene at end of Act Two requires simply a black drop and two baby spots to pick out priest and penitent, who are separated by the conventional screen. The voices of the other priests at confession are heard in the dark—the priests do not appear.

ACT ONE

ACT ONE

Scene i

The Community Room of the House of St. Gregory, in a small town somewhere in the United States—or for that matter in any country.

This is a vast room of lofty simplicity which would have become either Popes or Parliaments. Considering the history of the Order, the period might be any one of several—although modified Gothic perhaps best suggests the link with antiquity and the note of noble simplicity.

Essentially it is a great room, of stone with brown wood paneling if desired. Main entrance is a triple Gothic arch stage back, topped by a small black crucifix, the arch looking out upon a corridor which runs across stage back. Mullioned windows in this corridor look out on an inner court and up and down this corridor the House passes to class and to chapel.

Two great canvases dominate the room: stage right a massive painting of St. Ignatius Loyola and stage left one of St. Francis Xavier. A small staircase and landing upstage

3

right give access to other rooms in the house and against this landing, directly below the painting of Ignatius is a closed piano. On the top of the piano are some magazines and a candelabra. A square piano is preferable so pianist may sit with profile to audience and piano running lengthwise with staircase but a small grand piano will do, although in this event pianist must of necessity have his back to audience.

Stage left the side wall consists of a great Gothic fireplace, flanked by slim Gothic windows. Books line the walls upstage left and in the corner is a very plain Gothic bench with back. Downstage at fireplace is a comfortable leather chair.

A massive Gothic chandelier with candle-like bulbs hangs center above an eight-foot Gothic table, very plain, with six very plain chairs and two plain Gothic chairs with arms. The floor is a warm shade in suggested tiling.

The room has the mellow look of centuries about it but it is comfortable too. Downstage right there is a Gothic doorway leading to offices. The triple arches center are elevated above the rest of the room by a flight of three steps extending the width of the opening.

At the head of the long table is seated the REV. PAUL DUQESNE, S. J., *Rector of the House of St. Gregory, a slightly pontifical man of about 65 years—grey hair, ruddy*

*complexion. He occupies the head of the
table (or any chair in which he sits, for
Jesuit Rectors do not always take the same
chair) like the chairman of a bank board or
the president of an officers' mess.*

*In a chair near him going over papers, very
much the efficient adjutant, is the* REV.
CHARLES I. KEENE, S. J., *a lean, tall, hawk-
featured man of about 45 or 50.*

FATHER RECTOR *is opening his mail rapidly
and conversing briskly with the* REV. VICE-
RECTOR.

DUQESNE. [*Good-naturedly.*] Well, well—do people
never write except to ask for something?

KEENE. [*Crisply.*] What is it now?

DUQESNE. A speaker for a communion breakfast.

KEENE. Surely the Society of Jesus has more important
work than supplying speakers for communion break-
fasts?

DUQESNE. Oh come, Father Keene. Our work is anything that is for the *greater* honor and glory of God.

KEENE. But we are not getting anywhere!

DUQESNE. Father Keene, Time means nothing. How
far we went yesterday, how far we go tomorrow
matters little. We are merely instruments in the hands
of Almighty God.

KEENE. All this building. More colleges. More noviti-
ates. They used to call us the "militia of God"—mark-
ing time now, for what?

DUQESNE. [*Pointedly.*] For the good of your soul and the pleasure of your superiors. [*Then passing on to more mail.*] Oh, this is the day Father Quarterman arrives. Have you made the necessary arrangements?

KEENE. He is being met at the station.

DUQESNE. Good. Ah, Father Provincial is well pleased with our report.

KEENE. And what does he say about Blessed Joseph Martin?

DUQESNE. I find him quite favorable to the cause.

KEENE. [*Proudly.*] The Society has given many saints to the Church. It is time that one of the founders of this House is recognized.

DUQESNE. And the new novices? How have they been while I was away?

KEENE. They are as they should be—amenable.

DUQESNE. [*Smiling.*] Let us hope as much can be said for the fathers of the House.

[DR. PETER MORELL, *an aggressive confident physician, about 40 years old, enters through door downstage right.*]

MORELL. Morning, Dr. Duqesne. How are you, Father Keene? Well, how are you feeling today, Father Rector?

DUQESNE. Much better now that I am back. But don't tell me I need any more rest.

KEENE. [*Coldly.*] Early today, aren't you?

MORELL. Yes. I'm a little anxious about Father Sierra.

DUQESNE. Poor fellow. Is it critical?

MORELL. Can't tell. He's running a fever . . . and if he should get pneumonia! Well, three years on your back as a paralytic may be good for the soul but it's poor preparation for this kind of a fight. Wish I had him in a hospital but I don't dare move him.

KEENE. A pity—a fine scientist lost to the Society.

MORELL. [*Mockingly.*] And you don't bring out too many scientists, do you?

DUQESNE. [*Smiling tolerantly.*] No? I seem to remember Father Hubbard, Father Secchi, Father Haggen, Father Giafranchesi. . . .

KEENE. [*Coldly.*] One would think you had little faith, Dr. Morell.

MORELL. [*Airily.*] You know darn well I have none. That's why you put up with me as House physician! Nothing I hear or see can bother me. I have no faith to lose.

KEENE. [*Grimly.*] A pity you ever went to Loyola.

MORELL. [*Delightedly.*] So the Jesuits aren't good medicine for everyone? The Ratio Studiorum won't fit every soul?

DUQESNE. [*Genially.*] Come, come, Peter. If one or two mortals fail to fit into the sublime scheme of things, must we blame the divine plan?

MORELL. Oh, so it's divine. Well, how is every little thing with the Lord's Company this morning?

KEENE. Don't blaspheme, Morell.

DUQESNE. [*Kindly.*] Why do we annoy you so, Peter?

MORELL. [*With disarming candor.*] I often wonder. Perhaps it is your own estimate of yourselves, the grand assumption that as the last parade goes by, the Jesuits will be somewhere on the right of the line.

DUQESNE. [*Neatly.*] I trust we shall not be alone.

MORELL. I watch you in the morning going to Mass and in the evening on the way to benediction. And you seem always to be "at attention"—[*Softly.*] merely because down that corridor and in there before an altar where a little red light is burning, the Emperor receives what you think is His favorite company. Well, if you believe He does, maybe He does, but—

KEENE. How could you believe in us? You believe in so little.

DUQESNE. That is what we call faith, Peter. The Jesuits have no monopoly on it. Millions of other people believe the same.

MORELL. [*Quickly.*] But you're brilliant enough to know better. That's what gets me. You're like the intelligence section of a general staff. Yet you're a paradox. The great minds which you have you give to the Church with a particular vow of obedience that limits your use of them. I don't understand it.

DUQESNE. Is it so strange to vow obedience to the Creator of everything that lives and has lived?

MORELL. Maybe not. But what keeps you put? You all conform—so far as I can see—but what are you like

down inside you? What would you be if you were not
Jesuits?

KEENE. [*Proudly.*] There would be nothing else to be.

MORELL. I'm not so sure. I have you all placed. Father
Rector—the chairman of a board or a banker at the
very least.

DUQESNE. [*Smiling.*] No fair, Peter. You knew my
family. How about Father Keene?

MORELL. [*Starting for staircase stage right.*] Easy. He
was cut out for the Army—top sergeant, I'd say!

[*In the arch center appears the* REV. ROBERT STUART,
S. J., *Master of Novices, 50, a tall commanding figure
and a zealous Scot.*]

DUQESNE. And what about Father Stuart?

MORELL. [*On stairs.*] Oh hello, Bobby. Father Rector,
in any scheme of things how could he be anything except a shouting evangelist? [*Exits on landing.*]

STUART. [*Ponderously.*] Am I particularly amusing
this morning?

DUQESNE. You must not mind Peter Morell. He will
have his little joke.

STUART. [*Tartly.*] Too bad heretics can't have religion
as well as a sense of humor.

DUQESNE. [*Lightly.*] It might be worse if he had
neither. Well, out with it, Father. What is the bad
news? Surely there is bad news? Are the novices out
of hand?

STUART. It is not about the novices that I wish to speak

but about others. I consider it my duty as a loyal son of Ignatius to inform my Superior—in confidence—upon the variations in behavior of anyone in this community.

DUQESNE. [*Sighing.*] Very well. Proceed but make it brief. You always make me feel like the Secret Service!

STUART. [*Triumphantly.*] There is a spirit of unrest in the House. The seed of disaffection is being sown.

DUQESNE. Oh, is that all? That has risen and fallen like the tides, for centuries.

STUART. [*Vigorously.*] This is different. And it must not spread. I am not certain who started it but it is one of three members of this community—Father Rawleigh, Father Fulton or Father Ahern.

DUQESNE. [*Softly.*] The "three musketeers" of the Province.

STUART. Why should the three who most actively resist the habit of obedience have to be lodged in this House?

DUQESNE. [*Briskly.*] Specifically, what have you to report?

STUART. Let us take yesterday. Father Rawleigh went to town to conduct a noon novena to St. Francis Xavier. When you asked him last night how it went, Father Rector, he did not tell you he stopped to play handball on the way home, with a lot of youngsters from town?

DUQESNE. Oh come, Father Stuart, aren't we getting trivial? To be sure, he did not tell me. But I didn't ask him just what he did on the way back.

STUART. He concealed it just the same. As for Father

Fulton, when he went to town to visit the library, he spent part of the time at a symphony concert. Did he have permission for that?

KEENE. [*Sharply.*] He had permission only to visit his brother.

DUQESNE. Something must be forgiven Father Fulton on the score of music . . . you may remember that he gave it up under rather extraordinary circumstances.

STUART. He could play for us if he would, just the same. Then there's Father Ahern. Father Keene was assigned to censor a law article he was writing for the New Republic. When it came back with Father Keene's changes, Father Ahern refused to send it out.

DUQESNE. So? [*To* KEENE.] Was there anything objectionable in it?

KEENE. [*Suavely.*] Only the style. It did not seem to have our particular spirit about it, so I made—certain suggestions.

STUART. Which Father Ahern spurned. And just because he can not have his own way, he withholds the paper altogether.

DUQESNE. What reason did he give?

STUART. [*Crisply.*] He said that he, not Father Keene, had been invited to write the article. And in its revised form he felt that the article was no longer his. Said that at his first opportunity he would commend Father Keene to the New Republic—and the New Republic to Father Keene.

KEENE. There was no occasion for insolence.

STUART. [*With a Scotch zeal that touches you even while you smile at him.*] When is he going to learn that there is only one glory, the Order's glory?

DUQESNE. [*Pointedly.*] And—God's glory!

STUART. One of these three, I am sure, is on the verge of a break. What are we to do?

DUQESNE. But what have they done, really? These are small things.

STUART. It's small things that show which way the wind blows.

KEENE. I suggest that Father Rector question them.

DUQESNE. And resolve their doubts as a loving father with a confiding son? Hardly.

STUART. There is no time to lose. Disaffection spreads quickly.

DUQESNE. [*Firmly.*] Then it is decided. I shall put my trust in Father Ahern.

STUART. But he is suspect.

DUQESNE. Not by me. [*Softly.*] No, you are wrong about Father Ahern. Why, he has the feeling for The Great Adventure. Have you ever watched him when he preaches about the Society? He is like a painter aflame in the presence of a great canvas. To him we are The Divine Company—may we always be.

[*At the door downstage right appears the* REV. EDWARD QUARTERMAN, S. J., *tall, English, a man distinguished in the tradition of Newman. He is in street clothes of a distinctly English cut; the derby which he has in*

his hand is one with a high crown; and as a former
member of the Church of England he wears a monocle
without the least trace of self-consciousness!]

QUARTERMAN. [*Quizzically.*] Good-morning, Father
Rector. Do I intrude?

DUQESNE. [*Rising happily.*] Edward!

QUARTERMAN. [*Advancing and shaking hands center.*]
Paul! How good to see you again after—well, it must
be all of ten years.

DUQESNE. [*Warmly.*] You are Marco Polo come home
again. Fathers, let me present Father Quarterman who
is just back from India. Father Quarterman, this is
Father Keene.

KEENE. How do you do?

DUQESNE. And Father Stuart.

STUART. [*Shaking hands.*] The House is indeed hon-
ored. Shall I send Father Ahern to you now, Father
Rector?

DUQESNE. At once, please. I want him to meet Father
Quarterman.

[FATHER STUART *exits through door downstage right*].

KEENE. [*As* QUARTERMAN *takes chair at table, followed by* DUQESNE.] I hear they made you a bishop out
there.

QUARTERMAN. [*Diffidently.*] Oh, only while I was in
the Philippines. Now I'm just a Jesuit again, nothing
more, nothing less.

KEENE. [*Drily.*] But you weren't always. After all,

you were a bishop in the Church of England before you became a novice in the Society of Jesus.

QUARTERMAN. [*Smiling.*] You have no cause for alarm. I am content a Jesuit.

DUQESNE. [*Facing him from head of table.*] You return at the right moment, Edward. You are certain to be an inspiration to the House. You must come to the Recreation Hour after supper and tell us of India.

QUARTERMAN. It was not all adventure, Paul. So often glamour is merely the distance between here—and—there.

DUQESNE. [*Fervently.*] You have lived the life of Francis Xavier. You have gone into the far places. I almost envy you, Edward.

QUARTERMAN. [*Affectionately.*] Sentiment in the Father Rector! I enjoy new places of course but I think I love the old ones best. Can you guess what I did? I stopped off at Oxford on the way back.

KEENE. [*Now a tall shadow behind* RECTOR'S *chair.*] Can't you ever forget Oxford?

QUARTERMAN. [*Quizzically.*] Should I, Paul?

DUQESNE. [*Smiling.*] I guess we're big enough to love you, Oxford and all!

[REV. MARK AHERN, S. J., *40, vigorous and virile, the romantic intellectual of the Society, comes down the staircase stage right.*]

AHERN. [*Briskly.*] You sent for me, Father Rector?

DUQESNE. I want you to know Father Quarterman. Father Quarterman, Father Ahern.

[FATHER QUARTERMAN, *whose back has been to* FATHER AHERN, *rises eagerly and shakes hands.*]

AHERN. What tremendous good fortune! How long are you here for?

QUARTERMAN. [*Warmly.*] Indefinitely, I hope. I have always wanted to come to St. Gregory's for a long visit.

AHERN. Father Rector, we have corresponded for years but I had hardly hoped ever to have him here with us. [*Then to* QUARTERMAN.] Why you are almost a—well a fabulous personality now.

DUQESNE. What did I tell you, Edward? You will have the whole House at your feet.

KEENE. [*Drily.*] Let us hope that it will not result in a complete stampede for the foreign missions.

AHERN. [*To* QUARTERMAN.] Your letters always carried with them the flavor of Romance, of the Golden Age of Ignatius.

QUARTERMAN. [*Simply.*] I enjoyed my work. Simple fervor, simple virtue. It had none of your brilliance, Father Ahern.

AHERN. But I only write about things. You go out and do them.

QUARTERMAN. Yes, but you make canon law read like the gospels. Almost anyone can romanticize life in India!

DUQESNE. [*Smoothly.*] Edward, will you excuse me? I must talk to Father Ahern for a few moments. Father

Keene, will you have Father Quarterman shown to his room?

QUARTERMAN. Thank you, Father Rector. [*To* AHERN.] It's good to see you at long last. [*To* KEENE.] Your servant, Father Keene.

[KEENE *and* QUARTERMAN *go up steps center together and start left in corridor.*]

DUQESNE. [*Halting them for a moment.*] And oh, Edward—remember to be at your very best tonight.

QUARTERMAN. I shall not forget, Father Rector!

[*Exit* KEENE *and* QUARTERMAN.]

AHERN. [*Softly.*] He's just as I imagined he would be. Is that what Oxford does to a man?

DUQESNE. Oh, underneath he is no different from the rest of us.

AHERN. I'm not so sure. He has something more. Urbanity! That's what it is.

DUQESNE. [*Shrewdly.*] Urbanity? That means give and take. You're not like that, Mark.

AHERN. No, I'm afraid I'm all give or all take. Why can't we all be like Father Quarterman?

DUQESNE. He is the medicine that this House needs. Perhaps he can help you with what I want done. It's about Father Rawleigh and Father Fulton.

AHERN. [*Amazed.*] What have they done?

DUQESNE. I have reason to fear that one or the other may be near the breaking point . . . oh, nothing definite . . . but something is in the wind!

AHERN. That seems impossible. Surely I would have known about it.

DUQESNE. Well, perhaps nothing is wrong. But if there should be, save them for us. You have the flame, Mark. Make them feel it too.

AHERN. But isn't that your province, Father Rector? How can a man evangelize his friends?

DUQESNE. More than friends . . . don't you love them, Mark?

AHERN. Of course. But I feel so unarmed against them. And if matters were really grave, I might fail you miserably.

DUQESNE. [*Gravely.*] Whether we fail or whether we succeed, we are nothing except what we are for our God and our Order. Today I am a rector, yesterday Edward was a bishop.—Tomorrow—don't let Father Rawleigh and Father Fulton be outcasts tomorrow.

AHERN. Must it be entirely up to me?

DUQESNE. Why not? You are destined to be one of the great voices of the Society. You have the magic gift of tongues. Revive their faith. Make Father Rawleigh and Father Fulton believe that whatever may be bothering them is only spring fever—or anything —except what they think it is.

AHERN. [*Reluctantly.*] All right, Father Rector. If it must be I, it must.

DUQESNE. That's the spirit. Remember: nothing from without can ever hurt us. Nothing from within ever shall. There must be no break in the ranks.

AHERN. [*Starting for staircase.*] I shall do my best. I have no choice but to obey.

DUQESNE. [*Serenely.*] Just a moment, Mark. Please remember: the particular glory of the Society is that it *chooses* to *obey!*

AHERN. I shall remember, Father Rector. Is that all?

DUQESNE. Yes, thank you, Father Ahern. [AHERN *starts up staircase and the* RECTOR *stops him with a word that is not so casual as he tries to make it.*] Oh by the way, Mark, I just remembered. About that little article for the New Republic, you didn't mind, did you?

AHERN. [*With a flash of spirit that dissipates some of his humility.*] I suppose I should say: no, I didn't. But let me be frank, Father Rector. I love Fulton and Rawleigh as if they were my own flesh and blood. And so I shall do everything I can for them. But would it be too much to hope that the next time I might be permitted to write my own articles in my own way? [*Exits quickly.*]

CURTAIN

ACT ONE

SCENE 2

Father Fulton's room, a small cubicle which can easily be inset within the more permanent setting for the Community Room.

Through a casement window at one side you can see that it is spring; there are buds on the trees and forsythia are in bloom.

The room is nearly bare of ornament but full of papers and books, on the table, on the bed, on the floor. There is a plain door back center. A radiator cover at window is used as a bench and there is a plain couch bed against the other wall.

THOMAS RAWLEIGH, S. J., *an athletic, curly haired priest of 36, is lounging on the window seat, smoking a pipe.*

JOHN FULTON, S. J., *a tall, lean, aesthetic man of 38, who has lived much inside himself, is lying on the couch, head to audience.*

It is the interval just after lunch and both priests are smoking; FULTON *meticulously with the air of a connoisseur;* RAWLEIGH *jerkily.*

RAWLEIGH. A day like this makes you feel good just to be alive! Come on, smile—John; it's spring!

FULTON. [*Blowing rings.*] Is it? And what does Father Rector say to that? Now that spring has arrived, does he give his gracious permission for it—to continue to be spring?

RAWLEIGH. [*In high spirits.*] It slipped in on him by surprise. He has hardly had time to notice it yet. How about some handball outside this afternoon?

FULTON. [*Mockingly.*] Consider, my son: are you doing this for the good of your soul or the good of your body?

RAWLEIGH. [*Looking out window.*] I feel that if I don't let off steam today, I'll pull these walls down.

FULTON. And a new Samson was hailed in all the land. But where—where was Delilah?

RAWLEIGH. [*Softly.*] Probably old and fat now.

FULTON. And married?

RAWLEIGH. I don't know. Oh, smile if you want to: I guess I broke her heart. I got the idea when I was eighteen that everyone had to give up something of great beauty to the Lord. So I gave up Mary—and she me.

FULTON. I was luckier. I gave up my music to God but they keep wanting to give it back to me. [*Bitterly.*] Too bad, Tom, they can't do as much for you.

RAWLEIGH. [*Simply.*] Oh, I haven't any regrets. I've been happy in what I'm doing but every spring I get to thinking somehow about what might have been.

FULTON. [*Swinging to sitting position on couch.*] It's not spring. It's this place.

RAWLEIGH. Suppose—suppose it is. What could we do about it?

FULTON. [*Putting out cigarette.*] If I could find contentment, it would not be so bad but I can't.

RAWLEIGH. [*Straddling chair at desk.*] Strange, I thought everything was solved for me, once I joined the Society—like young people think it is when they first marry—what made us grow stale on the way?

FULTON. And we have to keep going. We enlisted for the duration of the war.

RAWLEIGH. [*Impetuously.*] Well, I'm tired fighting devils, real or imaginary. I'd like to go home. I want to be part of a real family again, that's flesh and blood of mine. It's pretty lonely being a soldier of God all the time. I want a furlough.

FULTON. [*Tensely.*] You wouldn't stop with a furlough. I know I wouldn't.

RAWLEIGH. [*Awed.*] John! You wouldn't dare desert?

FULTON. [*Sharply.*] Wouldn't you?

[*A knock on the door and* DR. MORELL'S *voice is heard.*]

MORELL. Hello. May I come in?

FULTON. [*Pleased.*] Morell! Of course. [*Opens door.*]

RAWLEIGH. We should have known it was you, Peter. Most people never think to knock in this House.

MORELL. Got a cigarette? Thanks. What do you do when you want to be alone?

FULTON. I'm surprised, doctor. Who should want to shut himself up aloof from his fellows?

RAWLEIGH. [*Lighting cigarette for him.*] If we were really nice, we'd leave the door wide open.

FULTON. But it's not every day that we entertain a heretic. Let it stay shut.

MORELL. [*Sitting on edge of desk.*] Not detaining you from class, am I?

RAWLEIGH. Wish you would. How can I get English Literature across to the novices I have? When they're not tragic about it, they're pious. Well, let them be pious in their prayers. What English Literature needs is a divine sense of comedy.

FULTON. You're lucky, Tom. I couldn't lighten their diet of Latin and Greek if I dared.

MORELL. [*To* FULTON.] You should be writing music. Lots of others can teach the classics.

RAWLEIGH. [*Mockingly.*] You forget: only the Jesuit can teach the classics!

FULTON. [*Sombrely.*] I didn't join the Society to write music. I could have done that out in the world.

MORELL. Some day maybe you'll tell me what people do join it for. I've often wondered.

FULTON. [*Abruptly.*] I'll tell you. I thought I wanted to be a martyr.

RAWLEIGH. [*Glibly.*] And die a martyr's death in China?

FULTON. I knew it would be a difficult life. But I wanted that. I chose to serve with the Jesuits like some men beg to be in the front line trenches. I wanted to be where the fighting was thickest. And I wanted to be a martyr. Can you imagine it? I a martyr?

MORELL. [*A little touched.*] Well, we all get strange ideas.

RAWLEIGH. [*Gently.*] Sometimes I look at my novices and wonder if their first ecstasy, like mine, must ever diminish. If we could only stay novices. . . .

FULTON. I remember my noviceship so well. I was on fire. I fairly walked and talked with God. And the master of the retreat suggested that I should give up something of me to God, something particular that nobody else could. So, I offered up what I loved most. I gave to God to keep for me the thing I loved most in life: my music.

RAWLEIGH. Why did you ever do it?

FULTON. Remember the sheer exaltation of your first retreat? I fancied myself a young saint of God. I had given up everything. And I did get something in return, something that lifted me up and kept my soul on high until—

MORELL. [*Sadly.*] There always seems to be an "until."

FULTON. One day a year after my first retreat, the Master of Novices came to me and suggested that I play at a concert being arranged for a visiting bishop.

RAWLEIGH. And you—refused?

FULTON. I refused. Oh, don't think I was just one more brave Jesuit standing out against some prince of the Church. I never felt less like a Jesuit. I told the Novice

Master that I had given up my music to God forever.

RAWLEIGH. What did he say to that?

FULTON. He smiled and tried to appeal to me as if I were in retreat again. "God takes and God gives," he told me and I told him: "God takes and *God can keep*" and I meant it. I have not touched the piano in eighteen years!

MORELL. I remember you so well: John Francis, the boy prodigy.

FULTON. I escaped that anyway. And I haven't always been bitter. It was a free will offering on my part. But every year since then I have been urged to play again and again. They keep telling me that every Jesuit must use the talents that are particularly his. But I hate them for tempting me. I was strong enough to make that promise. I am strong enough to keep it.

RAWLEIGH. Why haven't you said anything about this before?

FULTON. [*Sombrely.*] I never thought of doing anything about it—before.

MORELL. Say, I'm sorry I started all this. Maybe you'd rather I leave.

FULTON. No, it helps to have you around, Peter. You stay. [*Smiling.*] Almost refreshing to be making a general confession to a heretic. [*To* RAWLEIGH.] If I had said anything to you, it would only have disturbed you, Tom; and I knew you still found a song in life to sing.

RAWLEIGH. [*Musing.*] Did I? How little any of us know each other. If I have kept a happy face to the world, then I've fooled everyone including myself. I joined the Jesuits like you did, John, to do something big; only with me it wasn't exactly penance—more, romance, I guess. I could understand love and I began to believe that to love God was the only thing that mattered: the divine romance.

MORELL. [*Drily.*] But why the Jebbies of all orders?

RAWLEIGH. Imagination. I chose them like you do a hero in fiction. They just seemed to have more drama in them than any of the others.

FULTON. If it was only a part, you played it well, Tom.

RAWLEIGH. Of course I did because that's what it is, a part. Oh yes, Father Rawleigh is happy, Father Rawleigh is healthy, Father Rawleigh loves sports—his chin is up and his eye is clear. No maladjustment there, Father Rector. He's discovered the ultimate in life, he's a warbling minstrel of God! And why? Because Father Rawleigh still loves enough of the good things of the world to keep him sane.

[*The door opens and* FATHER STUART *appears.*]

STUART. I've been looking all over for you, Dr. Morell. . . . I should have known I might find you *here*.

MORELL. [*Slyly.*] Any objections?

STUART. Father Rector asked me to inquire what you think of Father Sierra's condition.

MORELL. I must observe him a little longer. That's why I'm still here.

STUART. Is there any change?

MORELL. There may be within a few hours.

STUART. [*Sweeping out regally.*] I shall see you later then.

MORELL. [*As* RAWLEIGH *watches* STUART *go down hall.*] What a bitter jest it would be if God turned out to be like Father Stuart instead of—

FULTON. Don't finish it, Peter. He's cast in God's image, even as you and I.

RAWLEIGH. You wouldn't rag him half so much, if he weren't so Scotch.

MORELL. Let a heretic have some fun, can't you?

FULTON. And by the way, Peter, how is José?

MORELL. Crisis tonight, I think. Tough case . . . on the verge of pneumonia. He has quite a fever. Little delirious too.

FULTON. Can nothing be done for him?

MORELL. José went through too much in the Revolution of 1931 in Spain. He came out of it with neuro-circulatory asthenia—what you call shell shock. And that complicates matters. Centers in his back and legs. With good luck I may break the fever. [*Tensely.*] I wish I *could* make him walk. Poor chap, he thinks he needs a miracle. I think all he needs is faith—faith in his legs.

RAWLEIGH. What business have you talking about faith?

MORELL. I wish it were my business. If I could take a little of the faith which the fathers of this House have

in their souls and put it into faith in their bodies, well—
I'd have much less business!

[*Knock at door and* AHERN *enters.*]

AHERN. Hello. Is Father Fulton receiving?

FULTON. Come in, Mark.

RAWLEIGH. [*Tensely.*] We're just starting to make
over the world. And we crave amusement. Tell us a
good story—if you can.

AHERN. [*Smoothly.*] If it's stories you want, come and
listen to Father Quarterman after supper tonight.

RAWLEIGH. Quarterman! When did he get here?

AHERN. Only this morning.

FULTON. One more diplomat, eh?

AHERN. He's more than that. He brings with him something that makes me proud that I am a Jesuit. Wait
till you hear him, Tom.

RAWLEIGH. [*On edge.*] I don't want to hear about the
heathen.

FULTON. I don't care where he's been. He hasn't been
through what I have.

AHERN. [*Candidly.*] What *is* the matter, John?

RAWLEIGH. [*Keenly.*] Who wants to know, Mark?
You or Father Rector?

FULTON. [*Quickly.*] Wait, Tom. That's a little rough
on Mark.

AHERN. [*Stunned.*] Father Rector did send me but—
you hardly leave me much to say.

[*The "three musketeers" are ill at ease and do not know how to proceed without hurting one another.*]

RAWLEIGH. Sorry, Mark. But the minute you came in, I had the feeling that you were the angel sent to speed us as we flee paradise.

FULTON. What did he ask you to do, Mark? Cast us out with bell, book and candle?

AHERN. I don't know where to begin. I can hardly believe it. I told myself it must be some silly rumor.

RAWLEIGH. Don't feel so bad, Mark—please. Why, you're only a step away from us. You weren't born to obey people all your life.

AHERN. You don't understand, Tom. You and John have things you love besides your Order. For me there is nothing but my Order—never was, never will be.

FULTON. Then it's good-bye, Mark. This is the jumping-off place. I leave tonight!

AHERN. [*Vigorously.*] Leave tonight? You're mad. You can't do that. At the very least you would have to write for your papers.

FULTON. Very well. I'll be regular about it. I'll write for my papers but I'll do it at once and I'll mail my letter to Father Provincial tonight.

AHERN. But where could you go if they did release you—you have no other home.

FULTON. I'll find a place somewhere. There must be some bishop who needs a good choirmaster.

RAWLEIGH. [*To* FULTON.] If you go, I go. Write if

you wish but let's not slip out quietly. I'd rather tell
them face to face what I—

AHERN. [*Sadly.*] How you love a good scene, Tom.
But it would be wasted. No one would try to hold you.

FULTON. [*To* RAWLEIGH.] Both of us shouldn't go at
the same time, Tom. Let me go and find out how it is
out there. If I am making a mistake, you don't have
to make the same one. Wait and see what happens to
me.

AHERN. You have it all figured out, John. But where
will you really run to? Isn't it inside ourselves that
things go wrong? How are you going to get away from
yourself?

FULTON. I don't want to get away from myself. I
merely want to be myself and I can't be myself here.
All these petty routines keep coming between me and
what I feel of God. They may be all right for those
who like to serve God in a strait-jacket but not for
me.

AHERN. [*Pityingly.*] And what about your vows?

RAWLEIGH. I made my vows too soon. Eighteen! Who
has a right to promise anything at eighteen?

FULTON. I am not worried about my vows. I can be
true to my priesthood.

AHERN. Will you both listen to me for just a minute?

FULTON. Nothing you can say will stop me.

AHERN. [*Simply.*] Can you remember the first solemn
high Mass we said together? I was celebrant, you, John,

were deacon and Tom was sub-deacon. It was a spring morning much like this. I felt then we were an eternal trinity, all for one and one for all.

RAWLEIGH. We were then, Mark.

FULTON. We never changed. It was something else changed.

RAWLEIGH. It simply wasn't so romantic as you thought, Mark. To us it turned out to be merely a lovely legend.

FULTON. You're dazzled by its brilliance, Mark. You could be a great lawyer out in the world. Why should you be a Jesuit? You loved the law once.

AHERN. Yes, I did. But the law lacked something. It taught me that for every wrong there was a remedy. In time I found out that was not so and then I realized I could only expect such perfection of remedy in divine law.

MORELL. [*Softly.*] And so you too joined the Jesuits —why them?

AHERN. Where else in the world is there anything like them? To me they are a canvas that is too big for one or two galleries, a panorama that takes four centuries to unfold. And I want to be part of the great portrait.

RAWLEIGH. All that means is you fell in love with the idea of the Order.

AHERN. [*Serenely.*] I do love it. I love its authority, its logic, yes, even its discipline. Oh, I may rebel now and again but in my heart I salute it for its sense of security, for its certainty of what is right. You see, my faith is a strange thing. I must have the feeling of men marching shoulder to shoulder with me: that's why I want to be part of the celebrated company of Francis Xavier.

FULTON. That's all right for you but I'm tired, tired going against everything my heart wants to do. I want to be the captain of my fate and the master of my soul.

AHERN. [*Simply.*] But you can't!

RAWLEIGH. Oh, can't we, Mark? It's so easy, it scares me.

FULTON. You think in images, Mark. Great pictures. Flaming canvases. Jesuits marching to conquest for Christ. Come down to earth. The Order is not the whole Church.

RAWLEIGH. We're only soldiers of fortune with a brain and a reputation, mercenaries in the service of the King.

AHERN. [*Flinging himself into his last great plea.*] If you're going to talk like history, read your Bancroft: "Not a cape was turned nor a river entered but a Jesuit led the way." Remember Marquette, Joliet, Carroll— and even today think of Edward Quarterman and India.

RAWLEIGH. No fair, Mark. Any man looks romantic against that background.

AHERN. [*Quietly.*] Then think of this. What is it that really matters in life? What is all the shouting and fury of living about? [*Very simply.*] Isn't it—to know God?

MORELL. [*Slowly.*] If there is a God, Mark, do you think He knows the Jesuits a little better than anyone else? Who ever said you were the King's Guards any-way?

AHERN. [*In summation.*] No one. But in a humble way I like to think that we are. If we can give or do a little more than anyone else, isn't that what matters? Isn't that the ultimate in life? And where can you find it if you leave all this? I can't pretend that I love every man in this House like a brother every minute of the day but I do know that in the morning when I raise the Host on high and in the evening when I hold the monstrance in benediction, I have more than Life itself in my hands. I forget then what I detest. I remember only that I am one of the Lord's Company and that nothing else in the world matters.

[*No one says anything. Suddenly the chimes sound outside for class. The spell is broken.*]

RAWLEIGH. [*Dully.*] There's the bell. Time for class.

FULTON. Oh, what's the use, Mark? I can't forget the people I hate.

RAWLEIGH. You make me feel so small, Mark—and that's what I am. I'm just not big enough. I'm going too, as soon as I can.

FULTON. No, you must wait, Tom, I insist.

MORELL. [*Preparing to go and a little disturbed.*] Queer. I had an idea no one ever left. You know, John, you may be lost out in the world, no matter how close you try to stay to your Church.

FULTON. I may be lost here.

MORELL. Of all people, I shouldn't be the one to stop

you, but remember, John : odd thing about folks out
there, they're not satisfied either . . . and sometimes
I feel about medicine the way you do about all this.
[*Exits.*]

[RAWLEIGH *tries to say something and does not; puts
on biretta and goes out.*]

AHERN. [*To* FULTON.] This is the point where in court
I used to say : counsel rests. But I don't, John. I'll never
rest while you feel this way. Surely there must be something or somebody that can make you see the truth.

FULTON. If only somebody could!

[*Chimes sound again and* AHERN *goes out;* FULTON
puts on biretta, picks up books and goes out.]

CURTAIN

ACT ONE

Scene 3

Community Room. 7:30 P.M. that evening. Candelabra on piano is lit and as curtain goes up you hear from offstage right men's voices with organ in closing bars of TANTUM ERGO, *which has been sung during scene change. At the "amen"* FATHER AHERN *enters, arranges a chess board at piano and is joined shortly by* FATHER RAWLEIGH.

RAWLEIGH. I had to take the chance of their missing us in chapel. I haven't seen John since this afternoon. Is he determined to send his letter tonight?

AHERN. Yes. Tonight.

RAWLEIGH. [*Restlessly.*] I should be doing the same.

AHERN. You're not cut out for a martyr, Tom. . . . I can't believe it yet. Things don't happen this way to us. They're not meant to.

RAWLEIGH. [*Bitterly.*] Why not? We're only human, aren't we?

AHERN. Yes, but we're something more too. If God gives us the grace to be His ministers, surely he gives us the grace to be masters of ourselves.

34

[*Offstage is heard organ recessional, the few moments that have elapsed suggesting the interval of benediction that follows* TANTUM ERGO.]

RAWLEIGH. Some of us aren't up to scratch, that's all. I hope John finds his place—somewhere.

AHERN. John has no place outside this House. He belongs here, if he only has the grace to know it.

[*Novices pass in corridor from stage right to stage left, as organ continues playing and in a few moments* FATHER STUART *enters with* FATHER QUARTERMAN.]

STUART. Yes, we still keep up the Recreation Hour, Father Quarterman. Fortunately that is one hour of the day when they have to be pleasant, whether they feel like it or not.

QUARTERMAN. [*Neatly.*] I had forgotten that recreation could be so official.

RAWLEIGH. [*Reading magazine at piano bench.*] You are a pleasant break in the monotony, Father Quarterman.

STUART. [*Down at fireplace left.*] Please, Father Rawleigh. Nothing is ever monotonous in the House of God.

AHERN. [*Bringing chess board to extreme right of table for a game with* QUARTERMAN.] An excellent quotation. I must remember it for a sermon some day.

STUART. [*Bringing paper to chair at fireplace.*] It is not a quotation. It is my own.

AHERN. [*Mimicking his Scotch accent.*] Well, Bobby

—it shows a profundity of thought that is overpowering.

STUART. [*Ruffled.*] Of this I am sure: where the House of God is, there is no room for humor.

QUARTERMAN. [*Smoking quietly as he studies chess game.*] Somehow I have always had the quiet hope down inside me that God has a sense of humor.

AHERN. I never could see why He should not enjoy a good joke.

STUART. Sacrilege! To talk of God as if He were the reader of a comic supplement.

RAWLEIGH. [*Thumbing magazine at piano.*] If we want to think of Him as a sublime humorist, why not? When you're on the altar Sundays, you're forever talking about Him as if He were a next door neighbor!

STUART. [*With a simple fervor very appealing even though you smile at his obstinacy.*] When I am out there, I speak as if He were at my elbow, because He is. When I am in here—

QUARTERMAN. [*Quietly.*] He is still here, is He not?

[FATHER FULTON *enters through center arch, hurriedly and a little nervously.*]

FULTON. Hello. I thought Father Quarterman would be telling some stories. [*Goes to piano and leans against it, reading a magazine, nodding to* RAWLEIGH *who is seated at piano bench.*]

STUART. We must wait for Father Rector.

RAWLEIGH. [*Smiling.*] I don't suppose Father Quarterman knows any forbidden stories?

QUARTERMAN. [*Moving a pawn.*] I am much more interested in what has been happening here.

FULTON. [*Not looking at him.*] Nothing ever happens here.

STUART. [*Suavely.*] That's because you live too much inside yourself. You must expand—you must get outside yourself.

FULTON. [*Significantly.*] Oh, must I?

QUARTERMAN. [*To* AHERN.] I liked your last article on "The Little Company." Are there to be some more?

AHERN. [*Drily.*] I think not.

STUART. Come, Father Ahern. Don't sulk. And I think you might write about something other than the Jesuits.

QUARTERMAN. Oh, I don't know. I like those on the Order.

STUART. We are too much in fiction.

RAWLEIGH. What Mark writes is not fiction.

STUART. Well—whatever it is. Why try to make the world understand us? It never will. Besides, why not write for a *nice* Catholic magazine for a change?

FULTON. [*Tensely—newspaper in hand.*] Look—Tom —tomorrow—Toscanini is giving his *farewell* concert!

STUART. I suppose you'll be there, if you get in to the city tomorrow?

FULTON. [*Meaningly.*] If I get into the city—why not?

STUART. [*Turning page of paper.*] Every time you go to the city you haunt some concert hall. Too much liberty spoils you. St. Gregory's doesn't offer you enough stimulus perhaps? I suppose you will ask permission to go to *tomorrow's* concert?

FULTON. You may suppose as you please.

STUART. We should all be able to forget the world.

RAWLEIGH. Why? I love the world. What's the use of pretending some of us hate it? It wouldn't be worth giving up, if we didn't like it a little.

AHERN. [*To* QUARTERMAN.] Checkmate!

QUARTERMAN. You have me.

AHERN. If life were only so simple as chess.

QUARTERMAN. It is, once you get to the point where in chess you say: I resign. There I do—and you win.

STUART. [*Deep in another paper.*] It's about time that the Cardinal answered Bernard Shaw and Bertrand Russell.

QUARTERMAN. Ah, now I know things are just the same. Do people still answer Shaw and Russell? The world changes so little. A few days and I shall be teaching the classics again. I have a new translation of the Odyssey with me.

STUART. [*Vigilantly.*] Has it been censored?

QUARTERMAN. [*Lightly.*] I trust so. It was translated by—Father General himself! I saw him in Rome on the way back.

STUART. [*Impressed.*] You should have told us before.

AHERN. Are you on some special mission?

FULTON. The General! I had almost forgotten he was real. [*To* RAWLEIGH.]

QUARTERMAN. I merely reported to him on my work. His office is as plain as a carpenter's shop. He is plain too. Speaks about twelve languages though—and looks rather like a musician.

FULTON. [*Softly.*] A musician? That's funny.

AHERN. [*To* QUARTERMAN.] I was afraid you might be an Official Visitor. And you might not find us at our best. Father Rector has been away for his health and we have all been under various strains.

STUART. [*Importantly.*] I am far from well myself. I don't know whom these first retreats are harder on: the novices or me!

FULTON. [*Half to himself.*] Poor kids.

RAWLEIGH. [*Mockingly.*] They tell me that you're pretty suave with them, Bobby. I must say you don't save much of it for us.

STUART. You should all be like them, like little children. They have no minds but God's mind and they are ready for us to mold them. That's what prayer has done for them in thirty days.

FULTON. Is that prayer? An endless questionnaire: five thousand questions and five thousand answers? Well, I can't pray that way any more. I have to pray the way I feel, not the way someone else wants me to feel.

QUARTERMAN. [*Quickly.*] Of course. Even Ignatius saw that. The Spiritual Exercises are to be undertaken on special occasions. There is nothing to stop you praying any way you choose, Father—

FULTON. [*Significantly.*] Thank you, Father Quarterman. That's about what *I* decided too!

[*In the arches center appears the figure of a parish priest—small, wizened, white-haired, shrewd. He is the* RT. REV. MONSIGNOR MICHAEL CAREY, *pastor of a parish nearby. He wears black street clothes, Roman collar, with purple of a Monsignor faintly showing at collar. He holds his place at the top of the steps for an instant.*]

MONSIGNOR. [*With a chuckle.*] Ah, my militant friends —good evening!

STUART. [*Barely looking up.*] Oh.

AHERN. Monsignor! Permit me—Father Quarterman, Monsignor Michael Carey.

MONSIGNOR. [*Happily.*] I am most fortunate—*Your Excellency!* [*Shaking hands upstage side of table.*]

QUARTERMAN. [*Smiling.*] Not Your Excellency, Monsignor. I am no longer a bishop now that I am back.

MONSIGNOR. [*Beaming.*] It's a pleasure just the same. I like to come in of an evening to gossip but this is a truly happy occasion.

QUARTERMAN. I confess, Monsignor, that I feel very much like a parish priest. That is what mission work does to one.

MONSIGNOR. But what is our work compared to yours?

QUARTERMAN. Something rather sublime, I think. After all, Monsignor, yours is the happy lot. You parish priests are like the patriarchs of old, one voice and one flock.

STUART. [*Droning from behind paper.*] Don't sentimentalize over him, Father Quarterman. You'll spoil him—and Heaven knows he's insolent enough now. [*Then as an afterthought.*] Sit down, Monsignor.

MONSIGNOR. [*Blithely taking chair at head of table stage left near* STUART.] Thank you, Bobby—kindly. Thank you.

STUART. Not in that chair. Father Rector often sits there.

MONSIGNOR. [*Impishly.*] Good. It will prick his vanity perhaps and that will be good for him. A bit of unexpected penance!

RAWLEIGH. [*Crossing from piano upstage side of table toward couch upstage left above fireplace.*] How are you, Monsignor? You're the cheeriest thing I've seen in weeks.

MONSIGNOR. [*Leaning back in chair and enjoying it.*] I'm quite well but then I always am. Tell me, Bobby: [*Slyly to* STUART.] How goes everything with the shock troops of God this beautiful evening?

STUART. I detest being called Bobby. And if you don't like us, why keep coming here?

MONSIGNOR. [*Blandly.*] We all have our weakness. Mine is a fondness of the foot soldier for the general staff. It must be that I like to be seen in the company of the brass hats.

FULTON. What is the secret of our appeal for you?

MONSIGNOR. [*Genially.*] Someone has to scold you. It might as well be I—I enjoy it so much. And besides you fascinate me a bit . . . perhaps I too should have been a Jesuit!

STUART. God help us.

MONSIGNOR. [*Airily.*] You'll pardon my delusion of grandeur? Oh, I admit I admire the simple magnificence of you at times. There's an aura of battle about you too but you're seldom in the front lines—except in the foreign missions. You have the headquarters air about you. You're miles away from the real fighting.

STUART. [*Bristling.*] Nonsense. We are not a military company.

AHERN. [*Amused.*] What would you have us do, Monsignor?

MONSIGNOR. [*Admonishing them as if he were Rector.*] Rub elbows with people. Oh, I grant you someone has to have the brains for general strategy and I admit you are masters of dogma . . . but the world doesn't go to pot on dogma any more.

QUARTERMAN. What is it that matters then, Monsignor?

MONSIGNOR. It's smaller things which most of you know nothing about. Smaller things make the breaking points—and you can't convert a sinner with a syllogism today.

QUARTERMAN. [*Cordially.*] We used medicine in the East.

MONSIGNOR. [*Delighted.*] Did you now? Then you know that the humanities are not so many words in a book of philosophy.

STUART. You talk as if we were an Order of contemplatives. We are not living in seclusion. We meet the world on its own ground.

MONSIGNOR. Yes, you do get about a bit, but what do you know, for instance, about living—and about dying?

FULTON. [*Despairingly.*] Who does?

MONSIGNOR. [*Simply.*] I saw a man die tonight. And this morning I saw a baby born . . . did any of you ever see a baby born? Let me commend it to your attention.

STUART. [*Stiffly.*] We are not a nursing Order.

FULTON. I haven't talked to a child in so long I've forgotten there are children in the world.

RAWLEIGH. My sister was here with her two boys last week. It must be fun to have a family growing up about you. . . .

MONSIGNOR. I used to preach a lot about birth and death. Then I saw a little more of both—and decided I knew very little about either.

QUARTERMAN. [*Admiringly.*] What do you preach about, Monsignor?

MONSIGNOR. Oh, I only say Mass now. I don't preach at all.

STUART. That must be a great comfort to the parish.

FULTON. [*Drily.*] Surely you haven't lost your faith, Monsignor?

MONSIGNOR. No. Merely my fondness for preaching!

QUARTERMAN. What do you do with the gospels, Monsignor?

MONSIGNOR. [*Wisely.*] I let them speak for themselves.

RAWLEIGH. Now that is almost an original idea.

STUART. I never heard anything so silly.

MONSIGNOR. I find it hard to improve on the gospels. They say all there is to say. And besides, I discovered that argument does not really change people.

STUART. [*Firmly.*] You would never have made a Jesuit, Monsignor. What about the appeal to reason?

MONSIGNOR. [*Triumphantly.*] What about the appeal to reason? Most people won't reason with you. And you know I don't really believe that the forces of evil are lined up against us like so many regiments, with the Dominicans assigned to take this sector, the Paulists that one and the Jesuits still another.

QUARTERMAN. [*Kindly.*] What *is* your theory, Monsignor?

MONSIGNOR. [*Simply.*] I have come to the conclusion that evil is personal, that no one can get at it except yourself and that nobody can do anything for anybody but himself. The best we can do is individually to approximate perfection—and if our example happens to influence somebody for the better, then that is a happy incident which can not be guaranteed in advance.

STUART. [*Impressively.*] Don't you believe in hell?

MONSIGNOR. [*All too meekly!*] Oh yes. There certainly should be a hell.

FULTON. You're right, Monsignor. Every man for himself—and his own soul.

STUART. And what about his Order?

MONSIGNOR. Soul first, Bobby—soul first, if you please!

[FATHER DUQESNE *and* FATHER KEENE *enter through one of the arches center.*]

DUQESNE. [*To* KEENE.] The singing in choir was a little ragged this evening, Father Keene. Attend to it.

KEENE. [*Drily—as he passes* FULTON *at piano coming downstage and taking seat on downstage side of table.*] Unfortunately these novices were chosen for their piety —not for their sense of harmony.

MONSIGNOR. [*To* KEENE.] It was always thus. You loaned me a tertian for high mass last Sunday and he couldn't sing a note.

DUQESNE. Ah, good evening, Monsignor—a pleasure. [MONSIGNOR *starts to rise.*] There, there, don't get up. Don't disturb yourself.

MONSIGNOR. [*Wickedly.*] Reverend Rector! Perhaps you are right. I am getting older and I should be careful. Therefore, I yield— [*Sinks into chair.*] gracefully, I hope!

DUQESNE. [*Taking chair on upstage side of table, next to* MONSIGNOR.] You have come in time to hear Father Quarterman tell us something about India.

MONSIGNOR. I am so sorry. I had no idea I was holding you up, Father Quarterman.

QUARTERMAN. On the contrary, we have been having a delightful time, Father Rector. I would much rather listen to the Monsignor.

[DR. MORELL *enters from door downstage right.*]

MORELL. Hello. Am I late for prayers?

KEENE. [*Coldly.*] Do you ever pray, Morell?

MORELL. No! Hello, Monsignor. I'm surprised to see you in this crowd.

MONSIGNOR. I could say the same for you. You haven't been to Mass in two years.

MORELL. Better give me up. The Jebbies did—long ago.

DUQESNE. Peter, I want you to meet Father Quarterman.

[QUARTERMAN *and* MORELL *shake hands.*]

RAWLEIGH. He's going to tell us what the Arabian Nights are like today.

AHERN. Won't you stay, Peter?

MORELL. Sorry. I came back to see Father Sierra.

DUQESNE. This is the third time you have seen him today. Is there any change?

MORELL. Well, frankly, I'm still worried. His fever is higher and he has considerable delirium.

KEENE. We were wise to anoint him.

DUQESNE. Do you think one of us should be with him?

MORELL. For the present I think it better for him to see no one. I will let you know if there is any change. [*Starts up staircase stage right.*]

FULTON. Oh, doctor—remember me to José, if you can—will you?

MORELL. [*In surprise.*] Why—of course.

FULTON. [*Interrupting him as he starts on.*] And, doctor—will you mail a letter for me when you go back to town?

MORELL. Certainly.

FULTON. I'll give it to you before you leave!

[MORELL *exits on landing.*]

DUQESNE. Poor José.

FULTON. [*Half to himself—at piano bench.*] I should think he'd want to die.

DUQESNE. Please, Father Fulton!

MONSIGNOR. But, my dear Rector, is it wrong for a man to prefer to die for God rather than to live for the Society? After all, who knows what God plans for us?

FULTON. [*Vibrantly.*] I'm glad I don't. I don't want to see my life spread out in front of me. I don't want to know what's going to happen. . . . I want to be surprised.

DUQESNE. Come, come—now we are getting moody.

[FULTON *starts to write letter at piano.*]

RAWLEIGH. Too bad you don't know a few good card tricks, Father Quarterman.

QUARTERMAN. But I do.

MONSIGNOR. [*Delightedly.*] Capital. I love to be fooled.

QUARTERMAN. Bring me a pack of cards some time and I'll show you. I learned from some of the best fakirs in the East.

KEENE. Is that how you converted the pagans?

QUARTERMAN. Sometimes! A good trick is often worth two good sermons—they usually understand the trick!

DUQESNE. We have delayed Father Quarterman unduly. Let's have it, Father.

QUARTERMAN. [*Standing at his chair, upstage side of table right.*] You speak in jest, Monsignor, but most of what happens in the East seems incredible. Sometimes it makes you wonder what there is in hypnotism.

STUART. Hypnotism? Bunk.

QUARTERMAN. Hypnotic suggestion then, on a vast scale. Out there you begin to believe that you have the power yourself.

KEENE. But that's sheer imagery, isn't it?

QUARTERMAN. I found that in some things Francis Xavier and Indian holy men like Mahatma Gandhi are not so far apart. They led the simple life and they had similar effects on people. They captured the soul by capturing the imagination.

STUART. I suppose you tilled the fields? We always get pictures of missionaries tilling the fields!

QUARTERMAN. [*Simply.*] We have to. You see, out there we don't put on religion like a Sunday coat. It has to be something that grows with the seed in the field, something they can see and touch. If you raise a good crop in the name of the Lord, not only the crop but your parishioners multiply. The natives think it's a sign from God—they believe in signs from God a great deal out there—they believe—

[*The luminous, tremulous figure of the* REV. JOSÉ MARIA SIERRA *appears on the landing stage right. A pale but shining figure, a shock of dark hair standing out against a cream colored dressing gown, he is almost an apostolic apparition. He sways uncertainly on his feet,* DR. MORELL *beside him, and advances to railing on landing in shaky but triumphant steps.*]

SIERRA. Deo gratias! Deo gratias! Deo gratias! Oh God, most merciful: *Behold,* Thy servant walks!

DUQESNE. [*Rising slowly.*] José! José! My prayers are answered.

SIERRA. [*In complete exaltation.*] God is good, Paul.

AHERN. [*Rising slowly in amazement.*] How did it happen, José? What does it mean?

STUART. [*Rising also.*] Glory be to the Father and to the Son and to the Holy Ghost.

KEENE. [*Standing—leaning forward eagerly.*] You were meant to walk again, José. The Society has need of you.

SIERRA. [*Looking straight ahead from landing and oblivious of* FULTON *who is at piano beneath him.*] John —John—where is John?

FULTON. [*Dazed.*] Here—here I am, José—what is it?

SIERRA. [*Slowly.*] The doctor said—you wanted—to see me—suddenly I saw that I could walk—and I knew that I could come to you . . . are you in trouble, John?

FULTON. You—you came down for me, José?

SIERRA. [*Serenely.*] I have been walking with God, John. And I saw many things I could not see before. I saw myself talking to—*Blessed Joseph Martin!*

FULTON. [*Looking up at him reverently.*] You—you mean you had a vision of the founder of this House?

SIERRA. [*Happily.*] Blessed Joseph told me to get up and follow him—and so I did. And I came straight to you, John. Now I know the meaning of those words— I am the Resurrection and the Life. He that believeth—

FULTON. [*Stunned.*] I do believe, José—I do believe. [*Dropping to knees.*] Your blessing, José—your blessing!

SIERRA. [*Raising his hands in benediction.*] Benedictio Deo omnipotentis, patris et filii et spiritus sancti, descendit super te et maneat semper. Amen.

[*The priests remain standing but bless themselves at point where* FATHER SIERRA'S *hand makes the sign of the cross.* MORELL *and* FATHER SIERRA *start down staircase,* AHERN *comes forward to meet and help.*]

STUART. It is a sign, nothing less!

AHERN. José! This is a great day for all of us.

DUQESNE. Now that you are returned to us, José—we are like one family again.

JOSE. [*Sitting weakly in end chair at right of table.*] Father Rector—the joy to be with you once more!

AHERN. [*As priests ply* JOSÉ *with questions and happy exclamations at table.*] What did you give him, Peter? [*To* DR. MORELL.]

MORELL. [*Leaving* SIERRA *and standing extreme right with* AHERN.] I gave him nothing!

AHERN. [*Vigilantly.*] But you said that all that was needed—

MORELL. [*Impressively.*] I did *not* cure him.

AHERN. [*Tensely.*] Well, if you didn't cure him, who did?

SIERRA. [*Turning gently from fathers at table and looking for a moment at* AHERN.] God did! Only God could. It *was* a miracle. I always said only a miracle could cure me and it did—it did!

DUQESNE. [*Softly.*] And through the intercession of Blessed Joseph Martin.

SIERRA. Suddenly my fever stopped. I knew I was meant to walk—I heard the doctor mention John—something commanded me and my body obeyed. . . . I heard a voice and I obeyed. I saw a sign and I came.

MORELL. We must go. He should go back to bed at once.

SIERRA. Please, doctor—I should like to pray. Might

we go to chapel, Father Rector? We won't be long, doctor.

DUQESNE. [*Coming to* SIERRA *and taking his arm with* KEENE.] Come, we shall recite the Te Deum.

STUART. [*Starting out to chapel through arch center.*] Now in truth this is God's House.

MONSIGNOR. [*Heading for corridor with* QUARTER-MAN.] We never heard your story, Father Quarterman.

QUARTERMAN. [*Going up steps with him.*] Monsignor, my stories are nothing. This is something that people can understand. In India it would mean converts by the thousands!

[*They exit right in corridor, following* SIERRA, KEENE *and* DUQESNE *to chapel.*]

AHERN. [*Halting* MORELL.] Look here, Peter—I don't understand it yet.

MORELL. [*Crisply.*] Don't try. [*Exits right in corridor.*]

RAWLEIGH. [*Joining* AHERN *on steps and going right in corridor with him.*] I feel as if I could shout for joy. You can't deny facts. Something saved us from going off the deep end.

[RAWLEIGH *passes on, while* AHERN *pauses to speak to* FULTON *who is sitting on piano bench, head on hands, leaning forward on the piano.*]

AHERN. [*Softly.*] Coming, John?

FULTON. [*Brokenly.*] You go along, Mark. . . . I want to be alone . . .

[AHERN *looks at him understandingly and exits happily toward chapel.* FULTON *has his letter to* FATHER PROVINCIAL *in his hand, clenched, as voices from chapel begin the Te Deum. After a moment or two* FULTON *tears the letter in two roughly and his hands drop accidentally on piano keys; the harsh sound awakens him, he fingers the keys idly, discovers what he is doing and starts again and stops. The impulse to play is strong upon him, there is a short conflict within himself whether to play or not but the surge of the voices off stage moves him and he begins the broad sweeping chords of the "exaltation" motif of a Beethoven Symphony. He makes a few mistakes at the beginning but stumbles along and in a few seconds catches the swing. Against the chant of the happy voices in the Te Deum his chords grow with majestic beauty and dignity. They soar quickly to a mighty peak and as the curtain comes down the candles burning so brightly beneath the portrait of St. Ignatius make of the piano a veritable altar.*]

CURTAIN

Note: *The Te Deum is recited by dividing the priests into two groups, with alternate lines to each group*:

Te Deum laudamus: te Dominum confitemur.
Te aeternum Patrem—omnis terra veneratur.
Tibi omnes Angeli—tibi Caeli, et universae Protestates:
Tibi Cherubim et Seraphim—incessabili voce proclamant:
Sanctus,
Sanctus,
Sanctus—Dominus, Deus Sabaoth.
Pleni sunt coeli et terra—majestatis gloriae tuae.
Te gloriosus—Apostolorum chorus,
Te Prophetarum—laudabilis numerus,
Te Martyrum candidatus—laudat exercitus.
Te per orbem terrarum—sancta confitetur Ecclesia.
Patrem—immense majestatis;
Venerandum tuum verum—et uni cum Filius;
Sanctum quoque—Paracletum Spiritum.
Tu Rex gloriae,—Christe
Tu Patris—sempiternus es Filius.
Tu, ad liberandum suscepturus hominem—non horruisti
    Virginis uterum.

etc.

ACT TWO

ACT TWO

Scene i

A week later. Community Room. At curtain: FATHER DUQESNE *pacing back and forth in considerable agitation.* FATHER KEENE *enters backstage center.*

DUQESNE. [*Decisively.*] Have you ordered the gates shut?

KEENE. Yes, but the crowds are increasing. [*Eagerly.*] We must do something.

DUQESNE. [*Thoughtfully.*] Yes, we must, but this is a Jesuit House of Studies, not a shrine!

KEENE. [*Pointedly.*] It could be a shrine. [*Smoothly.*] We did not ask them to come, it is true. But can we turn them away? If this is meant to be the beginning of a great spiritual renaissance, can we run away from it?

DUQESNE. But we must be sure. Was it a miracle that cured Father Sierra?

KEENE. [*Quickly.*] Are we sure it was not? Have you forgotten the cause for canonization of Blessed Joseph Martin?

57

DUQESNE. Is it your opinion that this was a miracle worked in his name—that this is the final evidence which we need to have Blessed Joseph Martin proclaimed Saint?

KEENE. It speaks for itself.

DUQESNE. Ah, if that should be. It seems to me I have worked most of my life for that. I thought I would have to be content with the beatification of the founder of this House. Until now I could find no miracle performed in his name.

KEENE. Can we refuse to examine the evidence at hand?

DUQESNE. No. We can not. But what will we do with all these people?

KEENE. There is a little altar at the tomb of Blessed Joseph. Let those who wish to, say a prayer—and then go.

[FATHER STUART *enters from backstage center importantly, sheaf of telegrams in his hand.*]

STUART. I've stopped answering telephones. But these keep coming. Photographers! Reporters! Moving picture people! We are on the first page of all the papers— St. Gregory's will be famous.

DUQESNE. [*Sitting in chair at head of table left.*] His Eminence, the Cardinal, may not be pleased.

KEENE. If the world comes back to us to do penance, inspired by a great miracle, shall we shut the door in the world's face?

STUART. [*Sitting down in chair between* KEENE *and*

DUQESNE.] The doctor does not deny it's a miracle. I have been talking to him.

DUQESNE. Well, if Dr. Morell believes, it must indeed be so.

KEENE. We have the evidence of Father Sierra himself. Can anyone look at him and believe that he has *not* walked with God?

STUART. The House itself has changed. Father Fulton and Father Rawleigh, with whom we had so much trouble, are new men.

DUQESNE. [*Impressively.*] Yes, that is true. All that has happened impresses me—we may be on the eve of —something.

[FATHER AHERN *and* FATHER QUARTERMAN *enter together center, as* FATHER FULTON *and* FATHER RAWLEIGH *come down staircase together. The priests take their places at table, obviously for a conference called by* FATHER RECTOR.]

RAWLEIGH. [*To* FULTON.] Did you ever see anything like it, John?

FULTON. No, it is certainly marvelous, Tom.

RAWLEIGH. I feel as if we were besieged by an army!

FULTON. [*In greeting.*] Father Rector.

QUARTERMAN. [*Smiling.*] It would seem that the Jesuits are popular once more.

AHERN. [*Taking chair at foot of table, stage right.*] Anyone suspected of having the ear of God would be bound to be popular today.

DUQESNE. [*Tolerantly.*] Oh, please, Father Ahern—why are you so eager *not to* believe?

AHERN. [*Pleasantly but doggedly.*] Why are you so eager *to* believe?

FULTON. When lightning strikes you, Mark, it never occurs to you to ask whether you believe in lightning!

[*As they are now spread about the table, they almost suggest the early fathers of the church engaged in momentous debate. Some are wearing their birettas, some take them off in the excitement of the argument.*]

DUQESNE. [*To* AHERN.] Surely you don't think the Society is a little less glorious if it happens to harbor a miracle?

AHERN. It was glorious without a miracle.

STUART. [*Getting up.*] Can't you forget, Father Ahern, that you're not a lawyer any longer?

AHERN. Not every unexplained cure is a miracle. If we have the word of God, we need no dramatic device to preach it. The Mass is everything, there can be nothing greater. This miracle, as you call it, will simply appeal to a sense of hysteria in people. And if we are not sure, how can they be sure?

KEENE. [*Pointedly.*] Once our Rector is sure, we *are* all sure.

AHERN. And are you sure, Father Rector?

[FATHER SIERRA *comes down the staircase: a changed man. He is still very much the mystic but also the recovered scientist; he holds himself differently and you*

catch the feeling of intellectual distinction now revealed.
He has several books under his arm.]

SIERRA. [*Taking place at table.*] Excuse me, Father
Rector. I am so sorry. It has been so long since I looked
through a telescope that I seem to forget the passage
of time.

DUQESNE. [*Warmly.*] You are forgiven everything,
Father Sierra. Now that you are back with us, we shall
expect great things of you.

SIERRA. [*Sighing happily.*] Sometimes I can hardly believe it is true. Why should God choose to let a miracle
cure me?

KEENE. So that you shall be the means of leading many
people back to the Church.

STUART. They are already at our doors!

SIERRA. [*Serenely.*] I knew they would be. At first I
wondered if it were a dream but it is all happening just
as he said it would.

AHERN. Who said it would?

SIERRA. Don't you remember? Just before I walked—
I saw—I spoke—with Blessed Joseph Martin. In the
cold light of day that may seem a little strange to you,
but I did. I did not just imagine it.

DUQESNE. Think, José. You are a man of science and
a priest of God. Was it truly revelation and not merely
an illusion?

SIERRA. You saw me walk. You saw the people come.
Everything has been done as he said it would.

STUART. Then we must let them in, by all means.

KEENE. It is a command which we can not ignore, Father Rector.

SIERRA. But of course you will let them in. He told me that too. There will be great pilgrimages in his honor and the House of St. Gregory will be a name hallowed through the ages.

RAWLEIGH. [*Impetuously.*] Father Rector, we should let them in at once. We must. Let us meet the world half way.

AHERN. But José, suppose you had imagined all this, while you were delirious.

SIERRA. [*Simply.*] I thought of that, too. So I asked Dr. Morell but he assures me that nothing but a miracle could have cured me.

AHERN. Couldn't he be wrong? Let us imagine, merely for argument, that it was not a miracle.

SIERRA. [*Smiling.*] Ah yes, I thought of that too. But you see, it is really very simple. If it was not a miracle, I would not have walked, would I?

QUARTERMAN. [*Quietly.*] Father Rector, have you considered: what will His Eminence, the Cardinal say? What will Rome say?

DUQESNE. I have considered that.

AHERN. You know the Church's position on miracles, Father Rector: the most severe tests are required.

STUART. [*Impatiently.*] Why do you keep putting obstacles in our path, Father Ahern?

QUARTERMAN. Have you considered, Father Rector, what it may mean to all of us to bring the world in here, to make St. Gregory's the cross roads of the world?

RAWLEIGH. [*Eagerly.*] What's the difference: whether we meet the world out there or in here?

KEENE. [*Half rising toward* AHERN.] And if it produces a new saint for the Society, if it means the success of Father Rector's life work, the canonization of Blessed Joseph Martin, would you still want to stand in the way, Father Ahern?

AHERN. [*Rising.*] Who indeed could stand in your way, once your minds are made up? Father Rector, may I be excused?

[RECTOR *eyes him steadily then nods his permission.* AHERN *starts out center.*]

SIERRA. [*Rising.*] But, Mark, it *was* a miracle! *I* ought to know.

AHERN. [*Turning at arch.*] If it is a miracle to you, José—all right. That's between you and God. But I can't see it. I can't feel it. And I just can't believe in it!

[*Exits quickly into corridor.*]

CURTAIN

ACT TWO

Scene 2

Community Room. Morning. Three days later. Seated at table checking records are DR. MORELL *and* FATHER FULTON.

MORELL. [*Passing index card to* FULTON.] John Ivancovich, age 11, Amsterdam: scoliosis and kyphosis with compensatory lordosis—improvement 30%. . . .Michael Morrisey, 62, Boston, congenital hip—improvement 25%; Mary Macy, 45, Albany, glaucoma, primary congestive, improvement 40%; Anna McGrath.

FULTON. Anna McGrath? She's from the village. Why, doctor, she couldn't hear.

MORELL. Of course she couldn't . . . but she does now.

FULTON. If this keeps up, we shall have to open a clinic.

MORELL. [*Gathering papers together.*] Keep those names for your records, Father. We will have a committee from the State Medical Society here to study the case histories. Later we'll ask these people to return.

FULTON. You think of everything, doctor. Why should it matter to you, a heretic, that these cases be certified as cures?

MORELL. [*Coolly.*] You'd never believe me if I told you.

64

FULTON. People are beginning to call St. Gregory's the American Lourdes.

MORELL. [*With some elation.*] There were one thousand people here yesterday. Today there will be two thousand.

[FATHER STUART *enters downstage right.*]

STUART. Good-morning, doctor. Any new cures today?

MORELL. Yes, a few.

STUART. [*Crossing to left.*] That's fine. That's fine. God's will be done.

MORELL. [*Picking up portfolio on piano.*] Will it?

STUART. It's stupendous. Why, only this morning I had six applications for the Novitiate.

MORELL. So even God's business picks up too? How many desertions do you expect?

STUART. [*Impressively.*] There are no desertions from the Army of God. Please remember, Dr. Morell, a miracle has touched this House.

MORELL. Yes. But I always understood that miracles were like a two edged sword. Some people they cure. Others—they destroy.

[FATHER DUQESNE *enters backstage center, accompanied by* FATHER KEENE.]

DUQESNE. Good-morning, fathers.

FULTON. Father Rector.

DUQESNE. How are you, doctor? You wanted to see me, Father Stuart? [*Sits at head of table stage left.*]

STUART. I hesitate to mention it, Father Rector, but the camera men want a picture of Father Sierra's room.

DUQESNE. That is quite impossible.

KEENE. [*Standing at elbow of* RECTOR.] A little unusual perhaps but there are times when pictures are more moving than rosaries, Father Rector.

DUQESNE. [*Firmly.*] There are limits. I do not mind the world coming back to St. Gregory's but I refuse to have it come within the very walls of the House.

KEENE. Perhaps they would be content with a picture of Father Sierra himself.

STUART. They already have that. They snapped it while he was praying at the shrine chapel yesterday.

DUQESNE. No, Father Stuart. Tell them my position is final. After all, we have been fairly liberal with the press—and they must be content.

[*Exit* STUART *and* FULTON.]

MORELL. [*Mockingly.*] They will never be content. They'll be with you at breakfast, they'll be with you at lunch and God help you, they'll even be with you at vespers.

KEENE. [*Coldly.*] A novelty for the gentlemen of the fourth estate.

DUQESNE. [*Wearily.*] Things are happening almost too rapidly.

MORELL. You must take better care of yourself, Father Rector. Remember that heart of yours. Just take things easy.

DUQESNE. It is a little bewildering at times. I feel as if the world has stampeded us.

[MONSIGNOR *appears in doorway downstage right, hat in hand and—deliberately—meek!*]

MONSIGNOR. Good-morning, my friends. Can you spare a blessing for a pious pilgrim?

DUQESNE. [*Cordially.*] Well, Monsignor—and how are you?

MONSIGNOR. [*Taking chair at foot of table stage right.*] I feel the competition!

KEENE. [*Stiffly.*] What do you mean—competition?

MONSIGNOR. [*Amiably.*] Every Monday morning I used to bank five hundred dollars from the Sunday collections. I hear you deposited twice that amount this morning, Father Rector.

DUQESNE. [*Smiling.*] The pilgrims *were* very generous.

KEENE. They were not from your parish, Monsignor. We are not poachers. You have nothing to worry about on that score.

MONSIGNOR. But how about you, my good friends? What is it going to be like for St. Gregory's to have a nice permanent congregation on its hands? Once you were chaplains extraordinary to the entire world. Now you become parish priests just like the rest of us.

KEENE. Would you deny the Society one more saint, Monsignor?

MONSIGNOR. [*Slyly.*] Oh, well—if you put it that way!

MORELL. When better saints are found, Monsignor, surely we may trust the Jesuits to produce them.

MONSIGNOR. You seem to be doing your bit, Peter.

MORELL. [*Coolly.*] One of life's little ironies.

DUQESNE. [*Rising.*] Come, Monsignor. A glass of wine will put you in good humor. [*Smoothly.*] And it has just occurred to me. You are a vicar forane, a friend of His Eminence, the Cardinal. You *could* say a word in behalf of our cause.

MONSIGNOR. [*Blandly—as he rises to face* RECTOR *across full length of table.*] And what should I tell His Eminence?

KEENE. Tell him what you have seen. At least you can believe that.

MONSIGNOR. I'm afraid I make a poor pilgrim. I find that vision adds little to faith. It is much easier to believe in things you never have seen. I find little comfort in what I touch and see— [*Pats vest in surprise.*] Sometimes I can hardly believe in myself. [*Blithely.*] Perhaps I do need that glass of wine, Father Rector!

[MONSIGNOR *exits back center with* FATHER DUQESNE *and* FATHER KEENE. MORELL *puts papers in portfolio, locks it, as* FATHER AHERN *comes down staircase.*]

AHERN. Peter—I have been trying to get you alone for a week. What is the meaning of these cures? Are they real? Can't medicine account for some of them?

MORELL. I treated José for three years and it did him no good.

AHERN. Don't fence with me. I want to know. Will all

the other doctors you bring here agree with your diagnosis?

MORELL. Just a second, Mark. You want me to tell you whether God modified a law of nature to cure these people? That's asking a lot. All I know is that most of them had faith which I could not give them. [*Coolly.*] And if that's a miracle, make the most of it.

AHERN. [*Doggedly.*] You are simply putting me off. I know the suggestive powers of faith healing once they are set in motion. But what put them in motion here?

MORELL. Don't you want to believe?

AHERN. I want to believe what is the truth.

MORELL. [*Shrewdly.*] And what is truth except what people choose to believe?

AHERN. Please answer me. Did you cure José, did he cure himself—or was it really God who made him better?

RAWLEIGH. [*Entering quickly downstage right.*] Mark —Mark—I've been looking all over for you. [*Very much excited, very much uplifted.*] Something extraordinary has happened. What do you think—who do you suppose is outside?

AHERN. Steady, Tom—steady—who is outside?

RAWLEIGH. [*With honest ecstasy.*] She is, Mark— Mary. And I never expected to see her again!

AHERN. Well—what is the matter? Why did she come to the shrine? Is she sick?

RAWLEIGH. [*Not stopping to analyze his feeling in detail but acknowledging the genuine and simple elation induced by the unexpected meeting.*] Sick? God no— she's—Mark—Mark—she's more beautiful than ever!

CURTAIN

ACT TWO

SCENE 3

Late same afternoon in the cell-like room of
FATHER RAWLEIGH. *Identical with* FATHER
FULTON'S *in Act One, except for a Vatican
print on wall and handball gloves and athletic
sweater on bed.*
On stage at curtain are FATHER AHERN *and*
FATHER FULTON, *who are waiting for* FATHER
RAWLEIGH.

FULTON. I wonder, after all these years, why she should
come back to St. Gregory's.

AHERN. Stop being subtle, John. What you are really
wondering is : what will she do to Tom.

FULTON. That's true . . . you know, I had forgotten
that women could stay pretty so long . . . but why
should he want to see her? What good will it do?

AHERN. [*Almost grimly.*] That is something you and
I know nothing about, John. You only gave up your
music—and I—I gave up nothing. I just grew up into
the Order. Tom gave up this girl and she gave up him.
God help them.

FULTON. But what have we to do with love?

AHERN. [*Drily.*] "Thou Shalt Love the Lord Thy God with Thy Whole Heart, Thy Whole Soul and Thy Whole Mind and Thy Neighbor as Thyself" . . . and for us that is supposed to be sufficient.

FULTON. Not quite specific enough for Tom. He has to lavish his affection on something personal but what can he do about it in any event? He is years too late. Consider his vows, her religion—what *can* he do?

AHERN. I wonder. At first I thought his seeing her again wouldn't mean anything very much but now I'm not so sure. . . .

RAWLEIGH. [*Enters slowly—takes off biretta.*] Hello . . . waiting to see me?

AHERN. [*Trying to carry it off lightly.*] Well, Tom, what was she like after all these years?

FULTON. [*Hoping to get him over the hurdle with a smile.*] Was she really the same girl you thought she was?

RAWLEIGH. [*Very quietly.*] Yes. She's the same all right.

AHERN. [*Alarmed.*] Tom! What *are* you going to do?

RAWLEIGH. [*Softly.*] I wish I knew. I'm all at sea. It's hell.

FULTON. But, Tom, I thought you were reconciled, just as I. Why should you want to change now?

RAWLEIGH. Hasn't a man a right to think of changing when he discovers—a little late—what it was he lost out of life?

AHERN. [*Sternly but not mawkishly.*] But you're not merely a man, Tom. You're a priest—of God. The mark of the Holy Ghost is upon you. You can't change now.

RAWLEIGH. [*Challengingly.*] Well then, if there is something in us after ordination that is bigger than there is in other men, why can't I shut my eyes to her and go my way?

AHERN. [*Crisply.*] You could if you wanted to, if you wanted to hard enough.

FULTON. [*Pityingly.*] Have you discussed it with her?

RAWLEIGH. I've said "hello" and "how are you"—and not much else.

FULTON. [*Hopefully.*] Then how do you know *she* still loves *you?*

RAWLEIGH. How do you know the sun is shining? [*Softly.*] Besides, she never married. You see, she made a promise too!

AHERN. What promise? A child of seventeen? None that was binding, surely. She was free.

RAWLEIGH. No. She was not free. She gave a promise for a promise, of her own free will . . . never to marry. And she hasn't. Now tell me that wasn't love, if you can.

FULTON. [*Awed.*] When was the last time you saw her?

RAWLEIGH. The day I told her I was leaving. I dreaded

the thought of telling her. But it was all right. If I wanted to give up something to God, she would too. So, two sentimental kids that we were, we made our promises—and walked out of each other's life.

AHERN. Did she expect to see you here?

RAWLEIGH. No. We never wrote. We literally stumbled over each other at the shrine and suddenly time seemed to play tricks on us. Today became yesterday—and it wouldn't be so hard, if she had changed or had not kept her word.

FULTON. Tom, you're thinking with your heart instead of your mind.

RAWLEIGH. [*Brokenly.*] I can't help it . . . it simply overwhelms me. What am I going to do? What is the way out?

AHERN. There is no way out. You closed that door eighteen years ago.

RAWLEIGH. At a pinch a man can always walk out of this House, can't he? How can I go on loving an abstract idea now? Oh, I don't say the Order isn't all right for some people.

AHERN. Such as?

RAWLEIGH. Such as you. It's simple enough for you, Mark.

AHERN. [*Sensing his own problems in future.*] Yes. Isn't it simple!

RAWLEIGH. With you it's the Order or nothing.

AHERN. Or nothing!

RAWLEIGH. With me it's different. Did I give my whole heart to the Society? Or did I leave part of it behind me out there?

AHERN. And what could you expect to find in the world outside worth jilting us for?

RAWLEIGH. God knows, Mark. I've prayed for grace to be able to say: don't be ridiculous, she can't matter that much, nothing can. But—

AHERN. Tom, come to your senses. Face this thing squarely. You are not free and you never would be. You'd be an outcast forever—think of yourself as an "ex-priest"!

RAWLEIGH. [*Desperately.*] I've said that to myself a thousand times but what if I don't belong here? What if I made a mistake?

AHERN. You could never be free of your vows. You can't turn back now. You're a priest forever.

RAWLEIGH. [*With disarming candor.*] But am I worthy to be so long as I feel this way? I can't go on unless I know I'm right. I can't wear this cloth with a lie in my heart. I'll have to put my Order and all its vows in one hand—and in the other everything else.

FULTON. [*Going over to* RAWLEIGH.] Tom, you can't throw away your life like this. Mark, you always see things clearly. You were very eloquent with me once— why can't you say something to stop him?

AHERN. [*Picking up biretta and preparing to leave.*] What more is there to say? This is Tom's problem and he alone can solve it. [*Puts hand on* RAWLEIGH's *shoul-*

der.] I pray God, Tom, that you don't go. But I have just discovered that the Monsignor is right. Nobody can do very much for anybody. And most of us can't do anything for ourselves.

[AHERN *goes out.* FULTON *looks helplessly at* RAWLEIGH, *tries to say something but does not and goes out.*]

CURTAIN

ACT TWO

Scene 4

Community Room. Next morning. FATHER QUARTERMAN *seated in easy chair at fireplace;* FATHER DUQESNE *walking up and down at stage right.*

DUQESNE. You seem to take events calmly, Edward.

QUARTERMAN. After ten years in countries where the impossible is always happening, I am prepared for anything.

DUQESNE. I suppose that the bigots will say: those Jesuit rascals are dealing in black magic again.

QUARTERMAN. [*Smiling.*] Fortunately our reputation does not depend on magic.

DUQESNE. I have decided. We must begin the cause for canonization at once.

[*At this point novices are seen passing back and forth in the corridor—also at other intervals—indicating some of the excitement and unusual tension which has been created in the House by the growth of the shrine.*]

QUARTERMAN. Have you a good postulator, a good lawyer?

DUQESNE. The best: Father Ahern!

QUARTERMAN. But Father Ahern does not believe in the miracle.

DUQESNE. He will believe. He must believe.

QUARTERMAN. Are you proceeding on the theory that the best lawyers are those who do not believe in the causes they plead?

DUQESNE. I know how to handle Father Ahern. He loves being a rebel. But he loves authority too. This will be a great opportunity for him. He shall go to Rome and assist in pleading the cause of Blessed Joseph Martin before the Congregation of Rites.

QUARTERMAN. If only everyone could be as sure of things as you are, Paul.

DUQESNE. [*Smiling.*] I have to be sure. It's expected of Father Rectors!

MONSIGNOR. [*Appearing in door downstage right.*] Good-morning, Father Rector.

DUQESNE. Oh, come in, Monsignor—come in.

QUARTERMAN. May I be excused?

DUQESNE. No, I want you to stay, Edward. I rely on your advice.

MONSIGNOR. [*Tongue in cheek.*] Father Keene will not like that!

DUQESNE. [*Eagerly.*] Well, Monsignor. What did His Eminence say?

MONSIGNOR. Hm . . . he was friendly—cordial as His Eminence always is—but he is not convinced.

DUQESNE. [*Pleasantly.*] He must be convinced.

MONSIGNOR. [*Blandly.*] How, Father Rector? He is not a Jesuit. You can not make *him* bow to *your* will.

DUQESNE. Does His Eminence forbid our activity?

MONSIGNOR. Oh no. You are in his diocese but he tries to let you manage your own affairs.

DUQESNE. [*Firmly.*] I will have Blessed Joseph Martin recognized as Saint. All I want is a free hand. Monsignor, I am tremendously obliged. Will you stay for lunch?

MONSIGNOR. [*Starting to go.*] No, thank you. I have some sick calls to make. I just dropped in to let you know.

DUQESNE. [*Walking with him to door downstage right.*] God will reward you for this, Monsignor.

MONSIGNOR. [*Amiably.*] Will he? I am not so sure of that!

QUARTERMAN. Why bother to assist us then?

MONSIGNOR. [*Genially.*] Vanity, Father Quarterman, vanity. I like to be with the winners. And somehow you Jesuits have the most consistent habit of turning up on the right side of things! [*Exits.*]

DUQESNE. [*Returning to table and sitting at extreme right of table.*] Why are people so reluctant to believe what they can see and feel? Well, they are going to let us have our own way. Let us be thankful for that. It is something.

[FATHERS KEENE *and* STUART *enter back center.*]

KEENE. The arrangements for the special novena are complete, Father Rector.

DUQESNE. Good. Then on Sunday we begin a novena of grace to guide our cause of canonization. And at the afternoon service I intend to announce the assignment of Father Ahern to prepare the cause for Rome.

KEENE. [*Coldly.*] Father Ahern?

STUART. Father Rector!

DUQESNE. *Y-e-s?*

STUART. Father Ahern, of all people! He is too much an individualist.

DUQESNE. [*Pleasantly stern.*] And so, my dear fathers, are you. I choose to tolerate a little of it in Father Ahern—but not in you—because in the end he will submit and do a great piece of work for the Society.

STUART. [*More humbly.*] And the opening novena sermon, Father Rector?

DUQESNE. Father Rawleigh will preach it. [*To* QUARTERMAN, *seated at table.*] He has a nice sense for the dramatic values.

KEENE. [*Daringly.*] And what is left for the third of the three graces—Father Fulton?

DUQESNE. [*Enjoying the thrust and pretending not to see it.*] Father Fulton will be happy to play for benediction, I am sure.

STUART. You have given the three major assignments to the three most troublesome fathers in the House.

DUQESNE. [*Grandly.*] So I have. And if the miracle

works that way on me, who knows what it may do to them? . . . Fathers, you are excused.

[FATHER KEENE *and* FATHER STUART *withdraw together.* QUARTERMAN *rises from table, leaves book near fireplace and approaches* FATHER DUQESNE.]

QUARTERMAN. [*Fondly.*] What a martinet you are, Paul. Sometimes I love you for it. Sometimes I hate you for it. Most always I admire you in spite of it. If you were not a Jesuit, you might even be Pope some day. But you are much too positive. [DUQESNE *smiles at the raillery.*] And they would be eternally afraid of you. For that matter, who could blame them?

[FATHER AHERN *enters back center as* FATHER QUARTERMAN *starts out.*]

QUARTERMAN. Mark!

AHERN. Edward! [*Then to* RECTOR.] I received your message, Father Rector.

DUQESNE. The opening novena, Father Ahern, will begin day after tomorrow, Sunday. Father Fulton will play and direct the choir. Father Rawleigh will preach the opening sermon— [AHERN *almost interrupts but restrains himself.*] and at the service I shall announce your selection, with the approval of Father General, as postulator for Blessed Joseph Martin.

AHERN. You can't mean that, Father Rector.

DUQESNE. And why not? You are the logical selection.

AHERN. [*Dazed and groping for words.*] I—I am not worthy of the honor.

DUQESNE. Nobody is worthy of anything, really. You

are chosen because the Society is worthy of your services.

AHERN. You compel me to be candid, Father Rector. I —I do not believe in this miracle.

DUQESNE. Then you approach the case with the true objective method of thinking. Your brief should be a masterpiece of logic.

AHERN. [*Vigorously.*] It would be far more logical if I were drafted by Rome to be devil's advocate upon trial of the case for canonization. How can a man plead a cause in which he does not believe?

DUQESNE. [*Eyeing him calmly and choosing to win the day on the simple question of authority.*] As your Superior I can not command you to believe in something that your soul rejects. But as your Superior I can and do request you to prepare for me the case in which *I* believe! [*Turns from table and goes up to steps at back where he pauses for a moment.*] And please remember, Father Ahern: when we pray at night to Almighty God, "Thy Will Be Done," it is not your will we speak of nor mine. It is God's will and who should know it better than the Society of Jesus?

[RECTOR *raises his biretta at word "Jesus,"* FATHER AHERN *bows his head, and* FATHER DUQESNE *exits right in corridor.* AHERN *shakes his head half in negation, looks up grimly at picture of St. Ignatius, then walks up and down restlessly, desperately attempting to map out a course of action. In a moment* FATHER RAWLEIGH *appears on the steps.* FATHER AHERN *crosses to him quickly.*]

AHERN. Tom! Have you seen Father Rector? Did he speak to you?

RAWLEIGH. [*Simply.*] I don't want to see anyone yet.

AHERN. Listen: there's to be a novena day after to-morrow. John is going to play and that's all right. But *you* are going to preach the opening sermon and *I* am to be the advocate for canonization. [*Bitterly.*] What a sublime joke!

RAWLEIGH. [*Happily.*] I'm not surprised. Nothing could surprise me now.

AHERN. What are you talking about? What has happened?

RAWLEIGH. [*With a new and different feeling of ecstasy—not the frenzied excitement of yesterday but the true contentment of a man who has been able to make up his own mind.*] As I started to say Mass just now at the shrine chapel, something swept over me. I saw all those pilgrims looking up to *me,* waiting to assist at my Mass, and suddenly I began to see things clearly. I knew then there is no other life for me but this and when I came down the steps of the altar, Mary was waiting to receive communion—think of it, Mark, waiting to receive communion from *me.* I shall thank God to the end of my days that I had made up my mind by that moment, that I was fit to give her the Sacrament.

AHERN. [*Lifted out of his despair for a second.*] I knew I was right, Tom. This is where you belong.

RAWLEIGH. After Mass we talked for a while and found

we made the same discovery. Don't you see, Mark, how it was? All these years we've been in love with an *image,* the image of a boy and girl who made a promise at eighteen! Well, we can write now if we want. We can see each other too—because we're going to hold on to that image and because it's just an image, nothing more.

AHERN. Tom, I can't tell you how happy this makes me.

RAWLEIGH. [*Softly.*] It's all linked up with St. Gregory's and what's happened here. Think of it, Mark: the only question in my life that could ever bother me is answered now forever . . . there *is* something here that shapes our lives whether we will or not!

AHERN. [*Now more than a little concerned.*] Oh, Tom —I only pray that this doesn't turn out to be merely some kind of shrine fever that touches you today and is gone tomorrow.

RAWLEIGH. [*Serenely.*] You don't have to worry about me, Mark. I'm sure now. I believe in all that's happened here because I feel it. I don't see why you don't— besides, can you prove it is not a miracle?

AHERN. [*In stark helplessness.*] No, God help me. I have to prove it is a miracle.

CURTAIN

ACT TWO

SCENE 5

*The stage is in darkness when the curtain
goes up and out of the dark you hear the
voices of various priests at confession. Their
faces never appear.*

DUQESNE. In nomine patris, et filii, et spiritus sancti.

RAWLEIGH. Bless me, Father, for I confess.

FULTON. It is one day since my last confession.

QUARTERMAN. I received absolution.

KEENE. I said my penance.

SIERRA. I confess to Almighty God and to you, Father.

[*The voices blend out in a murmur that fades to nothing as lights come on center and reveal* FATHER AHERN
*in his confessional. The purple stole is about his shoul-
ders and he is facing the audience. Kneeling at right
angles to the audience and separated from* FATHER
AHERN *by the usual confessional screen is* DR. MORELL.]

MORELL. [*In a frantic whisper.*] Don't you recognize
me, Mark? It's I—Peter.

AHERN. Of course I recognize you but we try not to

identify people. It's easier for them that way. What can I do for you?

MORELL. I didn't come to make a confession exactly— not a confession as you look at it. I haven't been to the Sacraments in years.

AHERN. What is it you want, then?

MORELL. I want to talk to you. I've got to talk to somebody. But first I want you to promise me something. [*Sombrely.*] I want you to regard everything I say in as sacred confidence as if I were making a real confession to you.

AHERN. I promise you that everything you choose to tell me I shall hold strictly under the seal of confession.

MORELL. You're going to hate me, Mark. I've done a frightful thing. . . . I've tinkered with something that's beyond me . . . it's run away with me. . . .

AHERN. Control yourself, Peter. Now what is it that is bothering you?

MORELL. [*Blurting it out.*] Don't you see, Mark? *José's cure isn't a miracle!*

AHERN. [*Aghast.*] I knew it. I felt I was right all along. [*Then like a lawyer on cross-examination.*] How could it happen? What brought it about?

MORELL. José had a dream, that's all. When he awoke, the ecstasy of it was still upon him. He forgot his emotional paralysis, the fever broke—and he walked. That's all there is to it.

AHERN. [*Grimly.*] No, Peter. That's not all. What's the

rest of it? [*Then more kindly.*] How could you do such a thing? I know you're not one of us but it isn't like you.

MORELL. [*With fleeting bravado.*] I always wondered about faith healing. Well, here was the chance to test it. All I had to do was let José think a miracle had touched him—and he was certain to walk.

AHERN. But why, Peter? Why were you willing to make fools of us all?

MORELL. [*Bitterly.*] I've hated the Society of Jesus . . . oh, I don't mean you and the others here particularly, but just all of you put together . . . and it amused me to think how some of them might behave once the world came back to them with so many of the things they had given up.

AHERN. [*Pityingly.*] And what did we ever do to you?

MORELL. What do you do to any man who has fallen away from the Church? Most of the time you annoy me . . . you make me feel as if you are all too good to be true.

AHERN. [*The relentless cross-examiner.*] The other doctors? How did you manage to deceive them?

MORELL. [*Mockingly.*] Did you ever hear doctors disagree on the diagnosis of an appendix? How expect all of them to be accurate in the presence of a *synthetic miracle?*

AHERN. [*Very much dazed.*] The "cures" continue—such as they are?

MORELL. [*Excitedly.*] Yes, but I forgot one thing.

What about the people who are disappointed? [*Shrilly.*] I never counted on that. I only meant to mock the Society. I never intended to hurt anyone else.

AHERN. Didn't you realize you could not hurt us without hurting others too?

MORELL. [*Fighting for coherence.*] Oh God, Mark. I forgot what it would do to children . . . they believe so hard. . . . Jimmy Magee, my sister's boy . . . his mother brought him all the way from the Coast . . . and *he believes* that he's going to walk. And he isn't, Mark. He can't. He isn't like José. Jimmy had anterior poliomyelitis when he was five . . . how can I tell him he isn't going to walk?

AHERN. That must be part of your just punishment: to let this poor boy see the truth.

MORELL. [*Brokenly.*] I can't, Mark. He's so sure. God —what have I done? What can I do?

AHERN. [*Vigorously.*] What can you do? There's only one thing to do. You will take steps at once to stop all these pilgrimages, as quickly as possible.

MORELL. And throw people into a panic?

AHERN. [*Grimly.*] No more of a panic than that of some who have made their whole lives over because of your miracle. [*Impressively.*] The Church does not live on error. You must tell Father Rector and those in authority and let it taper off slowly. You have done a terrible thing, a frightful thing, but thank God you have come forward in time to let me save my House—

MORELL. [*In outright revolt.*] I have done nothing of

the sort! I have simply come to you for advice—and I asked it under the seal of confession. *Don't forget that!*

AHERN. [*Note of terror in his voice.*] *NO.* No. No, Peter. You don't mean that. You can't mean it.

MORELL. [*In terror also.*] You are not to tell one word of what I said here. I had to talk, to someone I could trust, or—

AHERN. [*Speaking no longer as priest to penitent but flaying him as man to man.*] Someone you could trust? Why didn't you take your trust to someone else?

MORELL. I thought you were the right one to come to. You never were for the miracle.

AHERN. [*Bitingly.*] That's just it. Here I am the one person who could save this House and you bind my hands. You couldn't condemn a man to such a purgatory, Morell: to stand by helplessly and watch priests of God sanctioning such a blasphemy. I beg you: let me tell Father Rector before it is too late.

MORELL. Never. Never. It would kill José and God knows what it would do to Jimmy.

AHERN. Have you the faintest conception of what you are doing to me? Once you put upon me the seal of confession, I begin a living death.

MORELL. I can't help it, Mark. I can't tell and I won't.

AHERN. [*His despair mounting.*] Must I know the real truth of this all my life and say nothing? See my friends do the wrong thing and be powerless to stop them? Is there no pity in your soul, Morell?

MORELL. I must have lost my soul long ago. I'm only a feather tossed on the wind.

AHERN. [*Stingingly.*] And a white feather at that. I beg you—I command you—not as a priest to sinner, merely as one human being to another, let me speak the truth and save my Order.

MORELL. [*Piteously.*] All you think of is the Society. I'm thinking of kids like Jimmy who might never believe in anything again.

AHERN. [*Scathingly.*] And what do you leave me to believe in? I would rather you had plunged a knife through my heart. It would be far easier to die defending the seal of confession as martyrs have done than to live out this tragedy of error for the rest of my days. God help me, Morell—I can not even curse you, as I should.

MORELL. I'd pray, if I could, Mark, but I don't know what to pray for . . .

AHERN. [*Dropping to his knees.*] Morell, if you ever prayed in your life, you pray with me now—pray not for what you want but pray to God for what He wants. You have certainly put everything up to Him now . . . nobody else can do anything. . . .[*Then in great simplicity.*] Oh God, in whom all things begin and end, let Thy light shine upon us. Grant this man the grace to see the truth and the courage to speak it. Spare, we pray, these unfortunate people who keep coming here looking for something we are powerless to give them. Don't let this mockery continue, I beg of You— Show us the way, Oh Lord, or we perish!

[*The voices of the other priests in the dark are now heard—their happy, peaceful responses in Confession come up dimly at first near the end of* FATHER AHERN'S *prayer, and then more strongly. Between the last line of* FATHER AHERN'S *prayer and the curtain you hear these voices.*]

RAWLEIGH. "My God, who art all good and deserving of all my love."

KEENE. "I dread the loss of heaven and the pains of hell."

DUQESNE. "I firmly resolve with the help of Thy grace."

FULTON. "I ask pardon from God."

SIERRA. "—to confess my sins, to do penance and to amend my life. Amen."

CURTAIN

NOTE: *The responses of the priests above are extracts from the Act of Contrition which comes at the end of the Sacrament of Confession. The lines are deliberately not in sequence because we imagine we hear snatches from different confessions which of course would not have anything suggesting unison.*

ACT THREE

ACT THREE

Scene 1

Community Room. Sunday afternoon, the next day, about 4:30 P.M. From chapel are heard voices in the stirring hymn at the close of benediction: LAUDATE DOMINUM. DR. MORELL *is on stage alone at curtain. After a moment* FATHER AHERN *enters, sees* DR. MORELL, *thinks about going but stays and says nothing.*
Finally DR. MORELL *breaks the silence.*

MORELL. I rather thought you'd be in chapel with the rest.

AHERN. [*Tensely.*] I can't pray like pilgrims do at novenas, on the theory of do this for God or do this for that saint, and maybe they will do something for you. If people must pray, why can't they pray for the sheer joy of it?

MORELL. [*Involuntarily.*] It rather got me though, when they marched out to those exercises today.

AHERN. [*Near steps, looking down corridor.*] Sombre company on parade we Jesuits, eh! The Black Shirted Fascisti of God. No dress uniforms, no red hats amongst us—not even a domestic prelate.

MORELL. [*With an effort.*] See here, Mark. I can't have you thinking I'm a complete rotter. But I can't tell them what I told you. I can't.

AHERN. I can not even refer to the matter again. The seal of confession is final. No priest has ever broken it. No priest ever will.

MORELL. [*Pleadingly.*] I've started something and I've got to go through with it. People are coming here by the thousands every day. How could I tell them this all isn't so? [*Bitterly.*] I defy half of them to tell it from the real thing anyway.

AHERN. If only it were as easy to fool one's self.

[*The* LAUDATE DOMINUM *has been finished and the novices and fathers pass from right to left in corridor, while organ plays a recessional. The fathers enter the Community Room.* FATHER RAWLEIGH, *who has just preached, comes in quietly, nods to* DR. MORELL *and goes up staircase.* FATHERS STUART, SIERRA *pass in corridor with novices;* FATHER FULTON *does not appear, since he is the organist.*]

DUQESNE. [*Entering through one of arches center.*] Good-afternoon, Doctor. Ah, Father Ahern— [*A little sternly.*] I missed you from services this afternoon. I hope you were not sick.

AHERN. No. I was not sick . . . you said I was to meet you here?

DUQESNE. [*Eyeing him levelly.*] To be sure.

MONSIGNOR. [*Enters back center, a brilliant and happy figure in the mantelleta and rochet of a domestic prel-*

ate, wearing a black biretta with a red top.] Ah, Father Rector, this must be a very happy day for you.

DUQESNE. It was very nice of you to come over.

MONSIGNOR. [*Surveying himself humorously.*] Yes, I suppose I do add a bit of color to the occasion. But you know, I never get used to all this finery. I never wear it except when I have to!

DUQESNE. [*Affectionately.*] The Jesuit in you, no doubt. And now, Father Ahern, as I have indicated, I have made all arrangements. I made the announcement this afternoon. You are to begin the work of preparing the evidence for canonization at once.

AHERN. That is impossible. I do not accept. I can not accept.

DUQESNE. This is no time for modesty, Father Ahern.

AHERN. [*Desperately.*] It's not modesty, I tell you— it's—

KEENE. [*Standing with* MONSIGNOR *near* RECTOR.] I told you what would happen.

DUQESNE. [*To* KEENE.] Please! [*To* AHERN.] Father Ahern, I will speak with you alone. No, I want the doctor there too—and Father Quarterman.

KEENE. [*Propelling* MONSIGNOR *to door downstage right.*] Monsignor—

DUQESNE. [*To* MONSIGNOR.] Will you excuse me? Do you mind—

MONSIGNOR. [*Genially.*] No—I don't mind. I like being shoved around! Good-bye, Father Rector.

DUQESNE. [*Cordially.*] I almost forgot: won't you stay for supper, Monsignor?

MONSIGNOR. [*Pausing jauntily at door down right and eyeing the* RECTOR *speculatively through his glasses.*] Hm. Sunday? You'll be having cold roast beef. No, thank you. Besides, we're having ice-box cake tonight at the rectory—and your desserts are always terrible.

[*Sweeps out blithely, his biretta at a jaunty angle atop his shock of spike-like white hair.*]

MORELL. [*As* KEENE *exits with* MONSIGNOR.] Father Duqesne, you've been working too hard. You must not overdo. Remember what I told you.

DUQESNE. [*Sitting upstage side of table a little to the right.*] I shall remember, Peter. But I shall not obey you. [*Smiling grimly.*] No one gives orders here except me—and everybody obeys but Father Ahern. Sit down, Father Ahern.

AHERN. I prefer to stand, if I may.

[DR. MORELL *stands at extreme right,* FATHER QUARTERMAN *is sitting near fireplace.*]

DUQESNE. I wouldn't half mind you being so obstinate about the little things, like sitting down or standing up, if you were a bit more amenable about the bigger things.

AHERN. [*Hopelessly.*] And what are the bigger things?

DUQESNE. [*Proudly.*] Your God and your Order. But let's not fence, Mark. What was your real reason for not appearing at services this afternoon?

AHERN. I'm through. I'm finished. I can't stand this place.

DUQESNE. [*Wisely.*] How many times a day are people saying that to themselves, in every church, in every home?

AHERN. This is the first time I have ever said it. I wish no longer to be a Jesuit!

DUQESNE. [*Still choosing to be tolerant.*] You can cease marching with this Company, if you wish, Mark, but you will always be a Jesuit.

AHERN. It's no use, Father Rector. Your strategy won't work. You think to relax the reins a bit will bind me the more tightly. Well, it won't. Nothing you can say can touch me.

DUQESNE. [*Curiously—kindly.*] Tell me, Mark. Does it mean so much to your soul to have your own way? Is that what embitters you?

AHERN. No, I can stand having my life so dominated that every minute of the day finds me surrendering my will to that of my Order. I manage somehow to pray as you want me to pray, eat as you want me to eat, yes, even write for the magazines in the style that your censors would have me cultivate—but there's no—

DUQESNE. But what?

AHERN. There's no point to it. The bottom has dropped out of everything. This supposed miracle reveals us in a new light. We are only a regiment of straw men marching out to a sham battle. There is no enemy out there in front of us—and now I'm not so sure there is a—

DUQESNE. Stop, Mark. One word more is blasphemy.

AHERN. Then so is this miracle blasphemy. It is simply an outrageous hoax which—

DUQESNE. I think you had better explain.

AHERN. What have *I* to explain? Would it have interested this House so, had it not supplied the missing link in the evidence needed for canonization?

DUQESNE. [*Aroused.*] Do you imply for one moment that I perpetrated a trick upon this Community?

AHERN. No. You were sincere but you were wrong and then everybody followed you. Even the Church did not oppose you.

DUQESNE. You must apologize at once.

QUARTERMAN. Mark! The Church took no stand on the matter.

AHERN. But would it not have taken some stand, if any but our Society had been promoting this—

DUQESNE. [*Angry.*] You must be mad. There was no promotion.

AHERN. Not directly perhaps but you reasoned: this might be a miracle; therefore, let it prove itself.

DUQESNE. It has proved itself. Look at the cures we have had.

AHERN. Can't you see that most of the people who

come here cure themselves by believing in something that is not so?

DUQESNE. The doctor is the best judge of that. What do you say, doctor?

[DR. MORELL *and* FATHER AHERN *face each other across the figure of the* RECTOR. AHERN *of course can not force the question and answer, because of the seal of confession.*]

MORELL. [*Deliberately.*] You have nothing to worry about, Father Rector. Many of the doctors themselves disagree. Some think the cures are miracles; others think they are not.

DUQESNE. But the original cure, the recovery of Father Sierra?

QUARTERMAN. Is it your opinion that was a miracle, doctor?

MORELL. [*Slowly.*] I was the only doctor José had. I was the only one who knew his condition thoroughly before and after . . . his recovery will go down in the history of medicine as a miracle!

DUQESNE. There, Mark—you see.

AHERN. I see nothing but a ghastly mistake. I *know* it is no miracle.

DUQESNE. [*Quickly.*] What do you *know?* What is your evidence?

AHERN. I—I have no evidence.

DUQESNE. Be reasonable, Mark. I have been very patient with you, more tolerant with you than any

Father Rector need ever be with a subordinate. You have made amazing statements. I demand your proof.

AHERN. I have no proof.

DUQESNE. [*Losing temper.*] Can you expect me to rely on your intuition? We have the facts. How could they lead us into error?

AHERN. We could lead ourselves into error.

DUQESNE. [*Almost gently.*] Would God let us do that? With His grace, the Society "neither deceives nor is deceived."

QUARTERMAN. But you did believe in some miracles, Mark?

AHERN. [*Simply.*] Yes, I did. Christ performed miracles. So did Francis Xavier and I believe people are really helped and cured at Lourdes. But what has happened in this House I do not accept as a miracle.

DUQESNE. If you can't believe in this, what is it you have believed in all these years?

AHERN. I believed in all that really matters. I believed in Jesus Christ! [*Priests with birettas raise them.*] I believed that as I said Mass I was walking to Calvary with Him again and when He rose I stood with Him on that first Easter Sunday. Did I need to believe in anything else?

DUQESNE. [*Now truly alarmed at* AHERN'S *serenity.*] But if you are right and this was something less than a miracle, it would undermine the confidence of people in so many things. It would make them wonder if anything were real.

AHERN. Exactly. Now perhaps you can understand something of what it has done to me.

DUQESNE. [*Very much disturbed.*] Peter, tell me my faith in this miracle is justified. Tell me that Mark can't possibly explain it away, even to himself.

MORELL. Don't excite yourself, Father Rector.

DUQESNE. [*To* AHERN.] If you have any ground for your disbelief, it is your duty to reveal it to your Superior and if it is nothing you can put into words, what possible difference can it make to anyone?

AHERN. [*Sadly.*] It will make no difference to anyone. Let it just be that you believe one thing and I another. I shall be an outcast from my Order but it will still be the gallant Company before the world, touched by a strange miracle and admired by the entire Church.

DUQESNE. [*Shaking.*] If it is simply a question of faith, then my faith is as good as yours.

AHERN. But yours is only faith, whereas I know, in my heart—this is good-bye, Father Rector. [*Advances to shake his hand.*]

DUQESNE. [*Rising anxiously.*] You can't go like this. It isn't meant to be. You can't fail us now.

AHERN. It is you who are failing me!

DUQESNE. No! No! *God grant I am right!* [*Sways unsteadily on feet.*] *God make me right!* [*Falls forward on table as* DOCTOR, FATHER AHERN *and* FATHER

QUARTERMAN *rush to him, with a sharp cry from* AHERN.]

AHERN. Father *Rector!*

CURTAIN

ACT THREE

Scene 2

Community Room. Several hours later. The only light comes from the seven-branch candelabra which has been moved from piano to table; and from two holy candles on little stand, back of the couch which has been moved from upstage corner down near fireplace.

FATHER DUQESNE *is lying on couch which is on a slight angle. His head resting on a pillow is toward the footlights. Across his feet is a dark blanket. He is still in his habit.*
DR. MORELL *is upstage side of couch with* FATHER QUARTERMAN. *The other priests are scattered about the room;* MONSIGNOR *still in his brilliant red, the only note of color in the picture, is extreme right.*
The curtain goes up on the priests in prayer.

QUARTERMAN. Hail Mary, full of Grace,
The Lord is with thee.
Blessed art thou amongst women,
And blessed is the fruit of thy womb, Jesus.

PRIESTS. Holy Mary, Mother of God,
Pray for us sinners,
Now and at the hour of our death. Amen.

QUARTERMAN. Glory be to the Father and to the Son and to the Holy Ghost.

PRIESTS. As it was in the beginning, is now and ever shall be, world without end. Amen.

DUQESNE. [*Stirring faintly.*] Edward . . . Edward. . . .

QUARTERMAN. Yes, Paul.

DUQESNE. I thought I heard . . . prayers . . . for the dying . . .

MORELL. Don't talk too much, Father Rector. We thought it best not to move you.

[PRIESTS *rise to their feet now, but not together, one at a time.*]

DUQESNE. [*Gently.*] I remember. It is I—who am dying.

MORELL. Father Rector, you must be quiet.

DUQESNE. [*Smiling weakly.*] All my life I have talked when I could . . . I can hardly change now . . . have I been anointed, Edward?

QUARTERMAN. Yes, Paul.

DUQESNE. [*Serenely.*] I was right, Edward . . . there's nothing very much to dying. It seems to me that it's just like going from one room to another . . . only this time I shall see God face to face, at last.

QUARTERMAN. It is good to find you so happy, Paul.

DUQESNE. Yes, this is the day appointed, Edward, and I am content. I have practiced what Ignatius commended to the Society. I have contemplated death—looked upon it often—and I am ready. Father Keene! [FATHER KEENE *comes forward and kneels on one knee facing* FATHER DUQESNE.] You will be in charge, Father Keene, until a new Rector is appointed . . . use your authority with discretion!

KEENE. I shall carry on for you, Father Rector.

DUQESNE. [*With a faint shadow of a smile, dismissing him with a lifted hand.*] We shall see . . . Father Stuart.

STUART. [*Kneeling.*] Yes, Father Rector.

DUQESNE. Be tender with our novices—and try serving God with a smile for a change. You have a good heart, Robert, but don't be like— Edward, what was it Newman said about the Irish bishop?

QUARTERMAN. You mean the one he said had the intellectual outlook of a sacristan?

DUQESNE. [*Fondly.*] Exactly. How shall I ever be able to talk to God without you at my side, Edward? . . . Do be careful, Father Stuart, and don't forget to read your Newman.

STUART. Forgive me, Father Rector—forgive me. [*Drops back.*]

DUQESNE. Father Sierra.

[SIERRA *comes forward and kneels.*]

SIERRA. Yes, Father Rector.

DUQESNE. Pray for me, José. Pray for me by doing your best in science, for the Jesuit prayer is an active kind of prayer: the thing done is so much better than the thing said. Pray too that I have done right.

SIERRA. [*Humbly.*] You are always right, Father Rector.

DUQESNE. [*Smiling.*] Yes, it's a way Father Rectors have—but pray just the same. [SIERRA *drops back.*] And now let me see my "three musketeers."

[FATHER RAWLEIGH, FATHER FULTON *and* FATHER AHERN *come forward and kneel.*]

DUQESNE. [*To* RAWLEIGH.] Thomas, when I am buried, I want you to say my Mass. But no sermon . . . [*Gently.*] Oh, it's not that I don't like hearing you. But this time I wish you to talk to God for me and not to the congregation.

RAWLEIGH. It shall be as you wish, Father Rector. [*Drops back.*]

DUQESNE. [*To* FULTON.] John, of you I ask a special favor. There must be no mourning for me. And three days after my funeral about 10 o'clock in the morning, please go to the House chapel and play a small Te Deum for me!

FULTON. A Te Deum, Father Rector?

DUQESNE. [*Happily.*] Yes, a Te Deum—there is no death, only life everlasting.

FULTON. I shall remember, Father Rector. [*He withdraws.*]

DUQESNE. [*To* AHERN.] Mark, you and I have fought the battle of faith. And it is not over yet. I shall win in the end.

AHERN. [*Brokenly.*] I had so little to offer you and you counted on me so much . . . and now you have found something for everybody to do but me. It could hardly be otherwise.

DUQESNE. I shall ask nothing of you, Mark. You must be free, free to do as you wish. Let that be the farewell of one who loved you even while he fought you!

[AHERN *drops back and* MONSIGNOR *moves slowly across the room, the color of his robes a warming ripple in the scene. He kneels and bows his head at couch.*]

MONSIGNOR. And what would you have me do, Father Rector?

DUQESNE. [*Very much touched.*] Ah, Monsignor. You too a Jesuit to the end? Well, don't neglect them when I am gone. Come and plague them as you did me and I shall love you for it.

MONSIGNOR. [*Tenderly.*] I shall do my best, Father Rector. [*Withdraws and stands center at table, back to audience.*]

MORELL. I know so little about praying, Father Rector —it is I who must ask you to pray for me. . . .

DUQESNE. Ah, Peter. I loved you too. Mark . . . Mark. . . .

AHERN. [*Returning to couch.*] Yes, Father Rector.

DUQESNE. I . . . begin to see . . . the biggest miracle . . . is faith . . . *and to have faith is the miracle!*

AHERN. I have prayed for faith like yours but it won't come.

DUQESNE. It will. . . .

AHERN. I shall remember all my life, Father Rector, that you have shown us how to live—and how to die.

DUQESNE. No Jesuit is afraid to die. . . . The world must think us a queer lot . . . so many Warwicks devoted to an Invisible King . . . but if men give up their all to follow prince . . . or president . . . need we seem strange because we choose *God?*

MORELL. There, you must rest, Father Rector. You are tiring yourself.

DUQESNE. [*Gently.*] I am a little weary . . . I wonder: what will it be like to have someone else deciding things for me? What a battle life is in the fury to see whose will shall be done . . . but nothing matters, nothing except God's will . . . why can't people see that?

QUARTERMAN. You have helped many to see, Paul. You have fought a gallant fight . . . you have nothing to worry about. . . .

DUQESNE. [*Gently.*] Of course. "The Lord God is My Salvation. . . . Whom Then Shall I Fear?" . . . Come, Mark. . . . I have found something for you to do. . . . Let us pray together. . . .

[RECTOR *clasps his hand in* MARK'S *and the* RECTOR *leads his House in prayer: with* AHERN *scarcely able*

*to speak. The prayer they recite is the Creed and the
curtain comes down as they are about half way
through it.*]

PRIESTS. I believe in God, the Father Almighty,
Creator of heaven and earth,
And in Jesus Christ, His only Son, our Lord;
Who was conceived by the Holy Ghost,
Born of the Virgin Mary. . . .

CURTAIN

ACT THREE

SCENE 3

Community Room. Morning. Six days later.
FATHER KEENE *at head of table left;* FATHER
STUART *at his side; outside it is raining.*

KEENE. [*Opening mail as* RECTOR *did in Act One.*] Is
Mark Ahern in the House?

STUART. He expects to leave this morning, as soon as
it stops raining.

KEENE. If he must go, he must. . . . [*Smoothly.*]
Nothing that we might say could stop him.

STUART. Have you—er—ah—heard anything from
Father Provincial?

KEENE. Nothing yet.

STUART. We should hear something soon. Father
General will probably name you Father Rector.

KEENE. One can never tell. It might even be you!

STUART. I doubt that very much. If anyone has earned
it, you have. We need a Rector like you. You can't give
people too much headway. Look at Ahern. Does he
really dare to leave us?

KEENE. Yes, I think he does.

STUART. Where can he go? He might just as well leave the Church as to leave the Society.

MONSIGNOR. [*Appearing meekly in door down right.*] Ah, good-morning—my *vigilant* friends!

STUART. [*With a gesture to* KEENE.] You are addressing the acting Father Rector.

MONSIGNOR. [*Casually.*] My congratulations. [*Cautiously.*] Is it—final?

KEENE. We should have definite word soon.

MONSIGNOR. Would you mind if I visit your chapel? I should like very much to hear Father Fulton play this morning.

KEENE. [*Icily.*] Father Fulton will not play this morning.

MONSIGNOR. But Father Rector said—

KEENE. I am the Acting Rector now.

MONSIGNOR. [*A quaver in his voice.*] And the little Te Deum?

KEENE. This is no time for Te Deums. I shall not permit it.

MONSIGNOR. Would—would you object to my *praying* in your chapel?

KEENE. [*With a suave gesture.*] As you will—but tell me, Monsignor: why do you mock us so?

MONSIGNOR. Ah, my friends, if I mock you, I spare myself.

[FATHER QUARTERMAN *enters center, accompanied by*

FATHER FULTON, FATHER RAWLEIGH *and* FATHER SIERRA. QUARTERMAN *comes center upstage side of table between* KEENE *and* STUART; FULTON *and* RAWLEIGH *down by fireplace;* FATHER SIERRA *right with* MONSIGNOR.]

QUARTERMAN. You sent for us, Father Keene?

KEENE. [*Still seated at table.*] Yes. A slightly new routine, a new regime if you will, begins today. I am expecting that Father Provincial will—

QUARTERMAN. [*Handing him a cablegram.*] Perhaps this is what you are expecting!

KEENE. [*Dismay registering for a moment on a countenance that usually reflects no emotion.*] But this is a cable to you . . . and it's from Father General!! [*Exclamations of surprise from all the priests.*] It—it says that you are an *Official Visitor!*

STUART. [*First to speak in the murmur that follows the news.*] Father Quarterman an Official Visitor? Does that mean he has power over all of us?

KEENE. [*His poise recovered, he speaks coldly.*] Even over Father Provincial, if necessary.

QUARTERMAN. [*Quietly.*] Will you read the rest of the cable, please?

KEENE. [*Impassively.*] Father Quarterman is to take over the House; Father Sierra becomes Vice-Rector. [MONSIGNOR *touches* FATHER SIERRA'S *arm lightly by way of felicitation.*] Father Rawleigh becomes Master of Novices; Father Fulton is the new Prefect of

Studies—[*Amazement creeps into voice.*] And Mark
Ahern—

QUARTERMAN. Father Ahern, please?

STUART. What can Father General do with him?

KEENE. *Father* Ahern is transferred to head the new
Jesuit House—at *Oxford!*

STUART. [*Again speaking over the exclamation of the
others.*] But he is not one of *ours* now.

QUARTERMAN. Father Stuart, we speak a little too fre-
quently of what is *ours*. Nothing is ours. Everything
is God's and no matter what happens, Father Ahern is
a priest of God always.

KEENE. And what becomes of Father Stuart and myself?

QUARTERMAN. [*Judicially.*] Your severity, Father
Keene, almost tempts me to suggest that for the next
thirty days you make the grand retreat. But instead I
have decided to assign you to chaplain service in the
hospitals of the vicinity. You, Father Stuart, are
geared a little too highly for our novices. You and they
both need a rest. We shall assign you to library work
and I have decided also to loan you on Sundays to the
Monsignor, whenever he has need of you!

[*Startled glances are exchanged by* FATHER STUART
and MONSIGNOR.]

STUART. [*Looking straight through the* MONSIGNOR.]
An order is an order. I accept what is given me—but
I fail to understand how it could happen.

KEENE. [*Returning cablegram to* QUARTERMAN.] Very

well, Father Rector. I have nothing to do but submit.

QUARTERMAN. You and Father Stuart are excused.

[FATHER STUART *exits back center, followed by* FA-
THER KEENE *who gives a stiff inclination of the head
to* FATHER QUARTERMAN *by way of involuntary hom-
age.* MONSIGNOR *tiptoes up to arch and looks after
both, then smiles at* FATHER QUARTERMAN, *shaking his
hand a moment later.*]

MONSIGNOR. So! They're "changing the guard at Buck-
ingham Palace." My warmest congratulations, Father
Rector.

QUARTERMAN. You must always feel at home here,
Monsignor.

MONSIGNOR. A reprieve! I had the feeling that in another moment I would surely receive my walking
papers.

[*Chimes ring.*]

FULTON. It is time for the Te Deum. May I be excused, Father Rector?

QUARTERMAN. Certainly. We shall all attend. Father
Rawleigh, will you call the novices?

[FATHER FULTON *and* FATHER RAWLEIGH *exit,* FA-
THER FULTON *right toward chapel;* FATHER RAWLEIGH
left.]

SIERRA. [*In the manner of a petitioner.*] Father Rector!

QUARTERMAN. Father Vice-Rector.

SIERRA. For myself it matters nothing that I am Vice-

Rector but for St. Gregory's it matters everything now that you are Father Rector.

QUARTERMAN. Father Vice-Rectors have their place, José. They are as equity to the law. We need you to temper justice with mercy.

SIERRA. [*Eagerly.*] Then may I ask that in Mark's case you—

QUARTERMAN. José, your plea is granted before you ask it. I am ready to do anything within my power to hold him but there are times when the power of a Father Rector seems to be a very finite thing.

[NOVICES *pass left to right in corridor.* MUSIC.]

SIERRA. [*Simply.*] Sometimes I wonder why I should have recovered, if we are only to lose Mark as a result.

MONSIGNOR. [*Cheerily.*] Ah, José, sometimes it's hard to see the grand plan clearly. But there's always a reason for everything. And you do bring new hope to people, José. When they talk to you, they feel as if they had rubbed elbows with the saints!

SIERRA. That is the hardest part of all, Monsignor. Men see in me some of the things they expect from God. How to tell all of them not to hope for too much?

[*With a bow to* FATHER QUARTERMAN, *FATHER* SIERRA *exits center, joining* NOVICES. FATHER AHERN *comes down staircase in street clothes—but wearing his Roman collar—traveling bag in hand. He approaches table.*]

AHERN. Edward! I just heard the news—you an Official Visitor and now Father Rector? I can hardly—

MONSIGNOR. Ah, Mark—nothing in this life is incredible and almost everything about it is inevitable. Now who would ever have thought, for instance, that I should have Father Stuart for my own private chaplain! [FATHER STUART *is among group passing in corridor and* MONSIGNOR *looks up, catching* STUART'S *eye.* MONSIGNOR *swallows bravely and smiles at* FATHER QUARTERMAN.] Courage, Monsignor! [*Starts out center to join procession, then calls to* FATHER AHERN *from steps.*] Drop in and see me . . . some time . . . I shall always be glad to have you.

QUARTERMAN. Mark, I have good news for you. You are to be the head of the House—at Oxford.

AHERN. [*In complete amazement.*] Oxford! A month ago I could have hoped for nothing greater. Was that your idea, Edward, or Father Duqesne's?

QUARTERMAN. It was partly his, partly mine. We spoke about it often. He knew of my mission, you see, and—

AHERN. It's no use, *Father Rector.* I appreciate the honor but I can not accept.

QUARTERMAN. Paul was right. It is not easy to hold you, *Mark.* [*Inflection on the friendly* "Mark" *as compared with* AHERN'S *rather stiff* "Father Rector."] Isn't there anything that matters to you any more?

AHERN. All that matters now is: what is going to happen to that Magee boy? He's here now. He came with the doctor.

QUARTERMAN. Yes, I know.

AHERN. Well, can't you see that this boy closes my case

against you forever? He's the other side of the picture that I have been trying to tell you about. Surely you can't encourage him—

QUARTERMAN. I understand. I have spoken with the doctor and I told the boy it might be a little too exciting to go to chapel this morning. I said he could come in here and listen to Father Fulton play.

AHERN. Then you begin to see my point. What are you going to do with people who get themselves worked up to his pitch—and then find that nothing is going to happen to them?

QUARTERMAN. There is nothing for us to do. That part is up to God. It is not for us to say for how much or how little people should hope.

AHERN. Sorry—*in this case* that is just where we differ!

QUARTERMAN. Mark, suppose for a second that you are right. Would everything have to fail you just because *one* miracle failed of proof?

AHERN. [*Proudly.*] It would not be merely that. It would be my Order that failed.

QUARTERMAN. But your Order is not the Church.

AHERN. [*Softly.*] I never found out where the one left off and the other began. I only reached God through my Order. If that fails me, everything fails. I have no music like John, no feeling for living like Tom— I have only the Society of Jesus and if it goes, what have I left?

QUARTERMAN. [*Very simply.*] God is left.

AHERN. *Is He?*

QUARTERMAN. Mark, you frighten me.

AHERN. [*Bitterly.*] I frighten myself.

QUARTERMAN. [*Rising and going to him.*] What is it you demand of us—to believe in us once more?

AHERN. I demand nothing, Edward. But one of us is right and one of us is wrong. Of course it can't be you—[*Drily.*] You are His First Legion. But I say to you, Edward: if God is in His Heaven and knows what I know, how can He fail to intervene at once?

QUARTERMAN. [*Amazed.*] *Mark!* What is it you're trying to say?

AHERN. [*Sitting at foot of table right.*] Nothing. Nothing. I'm not trying to say anything. [*Brushes hand across head wearily.*] Don't mind me. I seem to go around in circles. I walk in them, think in them—even sleep in them.

QUARTERMAN. Must you go now—like this? Where can you go?

AHERN. With the Monsignor, if he will have me or with anyone who will take me in. I can stay here no longer.

QUARTERMAN. I can not bring myself to say good-bye.

AHERN. Do I need tell you what it means to me to say it? Here in this House I found peace and contentment. Why did I ever have to lose it here? Edward, some day when a novice grumbles because truth seems a little obscure, remind him for me how unhappy a man may be who has found the complete answer to every question.

QUARTERMAN. Will you walk as far as chapel with me?

AHERN. No, it would only make it harder to leave. I'll wait here until you're all in chapel and listen to Father Duqesne's *Te Deum*. Before you return, I shall be gone.

QUARTERMAN. Mark, there can be no good-bye between us. We corresponded for years before I came to this House. We shall continue to do so. Au revoir.

[FATHER QUARTERMAN *exits center and turns stage right toward chapel. Music stops for moment and then voices begin the* Te Deum. FATHER AHERN *is still seated at foot of table stage right. He does not hear the entrance of* JIMMY MAGEE, *a tow-headed youngster of 10, with the sparkle of great personality.* JIMMY *wheels himself in from door downstage right, very slowly, taking in the room with awe and considerable pleasure. And when he speaks, he has a disarming candor that is reverent even while it is colloquial.*]

JIMMY. Hello!

AHERN. [*Turning in surprise.*] Oh, hello. I never heard you.

JIMMY. Father Rector said I might wait in here. Say, I like your halls. I can go like the wind in them. [*Curiously.*] You—belong here?

AHERN. [*With an effort.*] No—I—do not.

JIMMY. [*Pleasantly.*] What are you doing here, then?

AHERN. I'm listening to a service for a man I loved very dearly—then I have to go.

[*Music dims a little from here on.*]

JIMMY. I like this place swell. It gets me! I asked Doc to bring me up here when I first came to town but Doc's been busy—or something. You know Doc?

AHERN. Yes, I know Dr. Morell.

JIMMY. [*Brightly.*] I guess you must know me too.

AHERN. [*Smiling in spite of himself.*] I guess I do. You're Jimmy Magee.

JIMMY. Mother brought me all the way from the Coast. I think the Jebbies—[*Corrects self with a smile.*] I mean—the Jesuits—are great fellows. Don't you think so?

AHERN. [*Warmly.*] No one ever thought so more than I.

JIMMY. Mother says they're just like Crusaders. No place on earth they don't go. Say, you must be one yourself. You look like one.

AHERN. [*Swallowing.*] I—have been.

JIMMY. They're going to let me make my first Communion at the shrine chapel tomorrow.

AHERN. Yes . . . the doctor told me.

JIMMY. [*Tensely.*] Did—did he tell you I'm going to walk too?

AHERN. [*Pityingly.*] No, did—did he say you were?

JIMMY. [*In a whisper.*] I guess he doesn't really be-

lieve it. But mother does and that's enough for me.
. . . I guess we got it all fixed up with God.

AHERN. Jimmy, even sitting in that chair, you have the
grandest thing in life: *Faith*. Don't ever lose it. And
now you know I'm not trying to discourage you but
we mustn't count on things too much.

JIMMY. [*Confidently.*] I'm not counting on anything
that hasn't happened here already. Lots of folks have
been helped and cured here, haven't they, Father?

AHERN. Of course they have, Jimmy, but not everybody.

JIMMY. [*Smiling.*] Maybe they don't all believe like
I do.

AHERN. [*Getting up and moving about.*] Jimmy, you
know about Lourdes, don't you?

JIMMY. I should say so. That's the place I've always
wanted to go to.

AHERN. [*Trying to decide how far he can go.*] Well,
they say at Lourdes that Our Lady touches those who
are cured but she smiles upon those who are not. So
remember, no matter what happens, God will smile
upon you.

JIMMY. You don't have to be afraid for me, because
I'm going to get better. I know it. I just feel it. . . .
[*Swings around in chair.*] Say, those must be the steps
down which Father Sierra walked, the night he was
cured! If I could only pray once—just once would be
enough—where he did the night it happened to him!

AHERN. [*Quickly.*] Visitors are not usually allowed in the sanctuary of the House chapel.

JIMMY. [*Wheedling.*] This is different.

AHERN. [*Turning away—and half to himself.*] Yes, Jimmy—God help us—this *is* different.

JIMMY. [*Wisely.*] You see, if God wants me to make my first Communion like other children do . . . if I'm really to kneel before His altar and not just sit up in an old chair . . . well it's like I said to Him this morning: Lord, I guess it's up to You; it looks like You got to do something about it—now—today!

AHERN. You know, Jimmy, it's not given to us to understand some things—but not everyone *can* be cured.

JIMMY. [*Grandly.*] That's what the kids in town say . . . but what do *they* know about it! [*Then with simplicity.*] Miracles happen. You can't get around that. Why, Father, didn't you ever see news reels of Lourdes? What about all those crutches? Somebody must have left them there.

AHERN. Of course they did, Jimmy, but this isn't Lourdes.

JIMMY. Everyone can't get to Lourdes and that's why God gave us St. Gregory's.

AHERN. Jimmy, I want you to be very brave about this. You *must* realize that even at Lourdes not everyone is cured. Some cases are harder than others.

JIMMY. [*With a wisdom not surpassed by theologians.*]

Oh, that's all right. Nothing is hard to God, particularly if you believe like I do—[*He looks up into the priest's face with complete assurance.*] And like you do, Father.

AHERN. It's because I want you to keep that belief, Jimmy, that I'm trying to make you understand you must not ask for too much.

JIMMY. I'm not asking too much. I don't expect to climb fences or run around the bases like other kids. But if I could only get away from this chair! If I could only do without this thing! That's not asking too much, is it?

AHERN. No, of course—[*Almost surrendering to the boy's enthusiasm.*] That's not asking too much. But *just suppose*—

JIMMY. [*Sombre for the first time.*] No, that's out. If it didn't happen just the way I know it's going to, something would stop inside me. . . .

AHERN. Don't say that, Jimmy. You must promise me: no matter what happens, you'll keep on hoping, you'll always have faith.

JIMMY. [*Smiling.*] Sure. I'll have faith all right. Fellows like me always have faith. It's about the only thing most of us have got—*but this time it's either sink or swim. . . . I win everything or I lose all I ever had!* [*His tension eases and he stops to listen; the music has grown a bit in volume and he notices it.*] Say, that's a keen tune. What's the name of it?

AHERN. It's *Te Deum.* [*Sun begins to shine through windows left.*]

JIMMY. Sounds kind of happy. What's it mean?

AHERN. [*Struggling for control.*] It means—"We Praise Thee, God."

JIMMY. Sure enough. That's just what it says. Almost lifts me right up out of here . . . please . . . couldn't I go to chapel with them this once? The music makes me feel like I could run to it—almost.

AHERN. [*Capitulating.*] You wait here. I'll ask for you.

JIMMY. Will you? You're a pal. And will you do me one more favor? [*Wheels over to him.*] Give me your blessing.

AHERN. [*Shaken by the boy's request.*] I don't know that I can give anyone a blessing.

JIMMY. Aw, please, Father, just for luck. I need all the help I can get.

AHERN. God love you, Jimmy; God bless you and God keep you. [*Raises hands together in first part of blessing.*] Benedictio Dei Omnipotentis, [*Then making sign of cross with right hand.*] Patris, et filii, et spiritus sancti, [*Then resting hands on boy's head.*] descendit super te et maneat semper. Amen. [*Exits right toward chapel.*]

[JIMMY *wheels up to steps to watch* FATHER AHERN *go down corridor; then wheels back into room, going over to staircase, where the sunlight is now upon him with full radiance. Offstage the* Te Deum *has actually finished and the organist has gone into a great melody which climbs rapidly. The boy smiles quietly, looks up as if listening and seeing—and suddenly he puts one foot ahead of the chair and then another and is literally drawn to his feet. He is facing the audience with an incredulous look of tremendous exaltation on his face, swaying unsteadily; he then manages an awkward turn toward the steps upstage and takes four stilt-like steps and pitches forward on his face in a faint. The music dims down from its great peak, just as* DR. MORELL *and* FATHER AHERN *come through one of the center arches in time to see the boy crumble.*]

MORELL. Jimmy. *Jimmy!* [*Rushes to him and examines boy, whom* FATHER AHERN *takes in his arms.*]

AHERN. The poor kid! Is he hurt, Peter—is it anything—

MORELL. [*Looking at his eyes and feeling pulse.*] He's fainted—that's all. Here, hold his head down a moment. He'll be all right.

AHERN. But, Peter—how do you explain it?

[DOCTOR *administers restorative.*]

MORELL. [*Joyously.*] I can't, Mark. It's beyond me. But he stood on those legs—and that's enough for me!

AHERN. Do you mean he—he's going to walk?

MORELL. Who can tell now, for sure? But you saw what happened—thank God I can face people once more. . . . [*Child stirs in priest's arms.*] Here, he's coming around . . . put him in his chair. . . .

JIMMY. [*Faintly.*] Hello, Father.

AHERN. [*Bravely.*] Hello, son.

MORELL. [*As they put boy in wheel chair.*] Don't try
to speak, Jimmy.

JIMMY. Speak? I want to shout! What did I tell you,
Father? *I got out of this chair! I'll do it again, too.*
I know I will. Please—can I—can I go to chapel now?

MORELL. [*Sitting alongside of boy and taking his
pulse.*] I think you had better rest a minute or two,
Jimmy. Just take it easy.

AHERN. [*Brokenly.*] You've done quite a lot for one
day, Jimmy.

JIMMY. Sure. Got to leave something for tomorrow!
Because I'm coming back tomorrow and the next day
too. I'll be looking for you.

AHERN. [*In growing humility.*] Will you, Jimmy?

JIMMY. Rather. You're my good luck. Why, say,
Father, this is just the beginning. And it's like I said:
it just *has* to happen, if you believe like I do. [*Brightly.*]
You'll see!

AHERN. I see now, Jimmy.

MORELL. [*Awed.*] Mark! It's just coming back to me—
what Father Rector said. Do you remember—the
night he—

AHERN. [*Slowly quoting the* RECTOR'S *statement.*] "The
—biggest—miracle is faith—and to have faith is the
miracle"—

JIMMY. I knew I was right all along. God can do anything! He can do anything He wants with me—and it's all right with me always!

[*The music begins to mount offstage and* AHERN *eyes the boy in growing wonderment, capitulating not alone because of the physical manifestation in the few steps taken but equally as much because of the boy's* supernatural certainty *that he will get better and better and the boy's sublime content with a hobble instead of a gallop. The sunlight is strong on the boy who is looking up with eyes shining; the doctor is sitting with bowed head at side of child and* FATHER AHERN *looks up into the sunlight as a man will when he meets his Maker or as Thomas must have looked up to the Lord. A wind rustles through the room and you feel definitely that Something has brushed your shoulders.*]

AHERN. [*Almost in a whisper.*] Peter—Peter—I never felt so insignificant in all my life—[*Then looking up above him.*] Forgive me— Forgive me—how could I have doubted Thee? [*Kneels simply at boy's chair.*] My Lord—and My God!

[*The music swells to a tremendous peak.*]

CURTAIN

KEY TO RECORDS OF MUSIC
MADE BY VICTOR COMPANY:
153 E. 24th St. N. Y. C.

PART I

First Section: Hymn to Ignatius, organ solo, used as overture just before curtain goes up on Scene 1 of Act One.

Second Section: Chimes meant to be used for tolling of campus bells but in New York production actual chimes were used.

Third Section: TANTUM ERGO, recorded by voices and organ, used between Scene 2 and Scene 3, with curtain going up on "Amen." After ten second pause, we repeated Hymn to Ignatius or brief Fourth Section for an offstage recessional.

Fourth Section: Brief bit of incidental organ music to be used as noted above or during any scene change. Usually Hymn to Ignatius or Organ Prelude in Second Section of Part II better for cover music.

PART II

First Section: LAUDATE DOMINUM, voices and organ, opens Scene 1 of Act Three, includes recessional on organ which is used.

Second Section: Organ Prelude used as fathers pass in corridor to chapel in Scene 3 of Act Three.

PART III

First Section: TE DEUM—actually only first third of full TE DEUM.

Second Section: TE DEUM—actually only last third of full TE DEUM. In the middle you dim out for about four minutes. Reason: record's length 4½ minutes; length of scene in which music needed 7 minutes.

PART IV

Made in one section. Organ solo, beginning at moment boy is left alone in Scene 3 of Act Three; climbs rapidly to peak for first minute, then dims as boy falls, continues quietly and is brought up with big surge at finish; for best effect use radio tube amplification.

Demco 292

Date Due